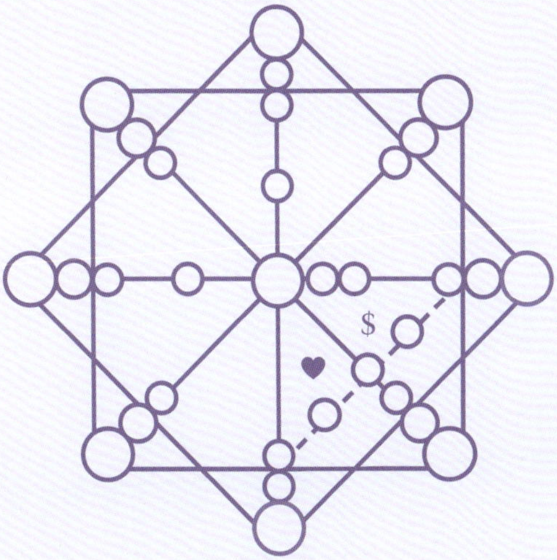

YOUR DESTINY MATRIX

To the wisdom of the ancestors.
To the forces that guide souls to awakening.
To those ready to heal their karmic programmes.
To the teachers and students of the Destiny Matrix.

First published in Great Britain in 2026
by Godsfield Press, an imprint of
Octopus Publishing Group Ltd
Carmelite House
50 Victoria Embankment
London EC4Y 0DZ
www.octopusbooks.co.uk

An Hachette UK Company
www.hachette.co.uk

The authorized representative in the EEA is
Hachette Ireland, 8 Castlecourt Centre, Dublin 15,
D15 XTP3, Ireland (email: info@hbgi.ie)

Distributed in the US by Hachette Book Group,
1290 Avenue of the Americas, 4th and 5th Floors,
New York, NY 10104

Distributed in Canada by Canadian Manda Group,
664 Annette St., Toronto, Ontario, Canada M6S 2C8

ISBN: 978-1-84181-683-8
eISBN: 978-1-84181-689-0

A CIP catalogue record for this book is available from the British Library.

Printed and bound in China.

10 9 8 7 6 5 4 3 2 1

Staff credits
Commissioning Editor: Louisa Johnson
Art Director: Jonathan Christie
Senior Editor: Leanne Bryan
Copyeditor: Vicky Orchard
Designer: Isobel Platt
Picture Research Manager: Jennifer Veall
Assistant Production Manager:
Allison Gonsalves

The information in this book is not intended to diagnose, treat, cure or prevent any disease, nor is it a substitute for professional medical, psychological or financial advice. Always seek the advice of a suitably qualified professional with any questions you may have regarding a health matter, other personal condition or financial advice.

YOUR DESTINY MATRIX

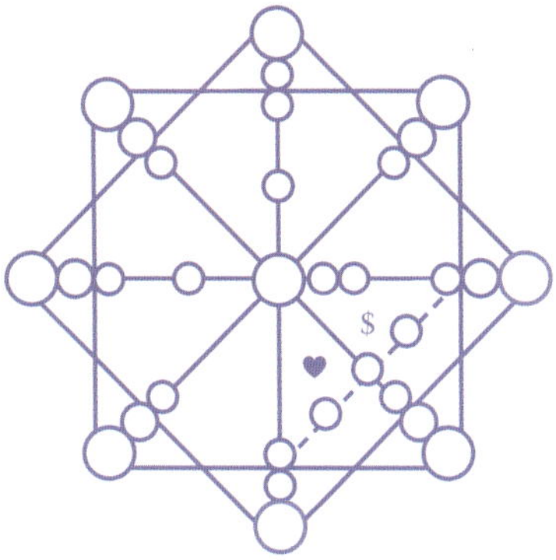

Discover your true path and embrace your purpose

KABITA GIRI

GODSFIELD

CONTENTS

INTRODUCTION

WHAT IS YOUR DESTINY MATRIX?

There is something greater taking place...

Your Destiny Has Begun

Have you ever sensed that your life follows a hidden pattern? That behind every choice, challenge and encounter lies a greater design? At times it feels as though invisible threads are weaving your story, guiding you towards lessons, growth and transformation. These threads are not chance or coincidence. They are the imprint of your soul's blueprint, written in symbols and numbers long before you took your first breath. This is where the Matrix of Destiny begins.

Your destiny may feel mysterious and distant. Yet it is already within you. It isn't fixed or limiting; it is a map of potential. When you learn to read that map, you can walk your own life path more consciously, align with your strengths, recognize your lessons and move forwards with clarity and purpose.

Your Destiny Matrix, also called the Soul Matrix or Purpose Diagnostics, is a system that helps you understand that personal path. According to this approach, you are born with a unique set of energies that influence your character, talents, challenges and overall direction in life, and these are represented by numbers. These numbers are calculated from your date of birth (see page 13).

This method of self-discovery is based on the idea that your birth date carries specific energetic vibrations. In esoteric traditions, 'vibration' refers to the energetic state of your soul, including the emotional, mental and spiritual layers. Your Destiny Matrix translates these vibrations into numbers that reflect different areas of your life, such as personal strengths, relationships, talents, health, finances, family patterns, life goals, soul missions and overall purpose.

People born on the same date share the same Destiny Matrix, but this doesn't mean they live the same life or have the same personality. Individual experiences are shaped by many factors, including family, culture, environment and, most importantly, choices. For this reason, your Destiny Matrix doesn't limit you or predict a fixed future. Instead, it serves as a tool for self-awareness, helping you to recognize your inner resources and align more consciously with your life direction.

History of the Matrix

The Destiny Matrix method became widely known in the early 2000s and was developed by Natalia Ladini, a numerologist, healer, Reiki master and spiritual teacher. She is the author of several bestselling books on destiny, numerology and karma, and the creator of the method Diagnosis of Purpose: The Matrix of Destiny.

Through years of spiritual practice, meditation, travel to sacred places and work with people, Ladini developed a structured system for calculating and interpreting how 22 universal energies, representing core qualities of life, consciousness and human development, operate in life. These energies correspond to the 22 Major Arcana of the Tarot, which symbolically describe stages of personal and spiritual growth.

Each of the 22 energies can be expressed in different ways, ranging from challenging to supportive, and relate to different forms of karma: personal, ancestral, collective and even planetary. Your destiny reflects the goals of your soul, which has entered this life to learn specific lessons and continue its spiritual evolution. All of this information is believed to be encoded in your date of birth.

What Does Your Destiny Matrix Show?

Your Destiny Matrix can give insight into the following areas:

- **Character:** Your Destiny Matrix shows your personal traits, behaviour patterns and how you interact with others.
- **Parent–child relationships:** It reveals possible challenges between parents and children and suggests ways to improve understanding and harmony.
- **Gifts:** It helps identify your natural abilities and strengths, making it easier for you to choose the right direction for growth and self-realization.
- **Lessons and karmic tasks:** It shows unresolved karmic issues from the past and your soul's main lessons in your current life.
- **Material tasks:** It highlights how past-life patterns may be affecting your financial potential, along with ways to move beyond them.
- **Health:** It provides an energetic view of health, including chakra balance and how unresolved family karmic patterns may be affecting your energy levels, and offers guidance on maintaining your well-being.
- **Love and relationships:** It explains your emotional needs, relationship dynamics, the type of partner you are compatible with and your shared goals.
- **Finances:** It reveals your financial potential, the ways of earning money that are suitable for you and the areas in which you can welcome in prosperity.
- **Purpose:** It helps you understand your personal, social and spiritual purpose and the key tasks involved.
- **Life cycles and yearly forecasts:** It shows the energies influencing different years of your life and the themes or challenges that may arise during certain periods.

How to Use This Book

To manually calculate your personal Destiny Matrix, see page 13. If you prefer a quicker option, you may generate your Destiny Matrix chart online using a free calculator; simply search for 'Destiny Matrix chart' or use the link below:

codingnumerology-matrix.netlify.app/

Once you have your chart, return to this book and follow the chapters in order, applying the interpretations to your own Destiny Matrix as you read. The pages that follow will guide you step by step through the structure of your Matrix and the meanings behind its energies, before showing you how to read and apply this knowledge in your own life. You don't need prior experience with numerology, Tarot or spiritual systems, only trust and openness.

As you move through this book, allow yourself to reflect, notice patterns and connect the insights to your life. Each chapter builds on the last, helping you uncover how your Matrix is formed and how its patterns express themselves in your character, relationships, challenges and purpose. Take your time as you read and return to sections whenever you feel called to do so.

This system is a tool for reflection rather than a rulebook. Understanding your Destiny Matrix can help you gain clarity about your strengths, challenges and life direction, and is especially helpful if you are feeling uncertain, confused or disconnected from your path. Rather than limiting you, the Destiny Matrix encourages self-understanding, confidence and conscious growth on both a personal and spiritual level. You are invited to meet it with curiosity rather than certainty, using it to gain insight while remaining grounded in your own free will, choices and lived experience.

Now, go ahead and turn the page – your destiny awaits.

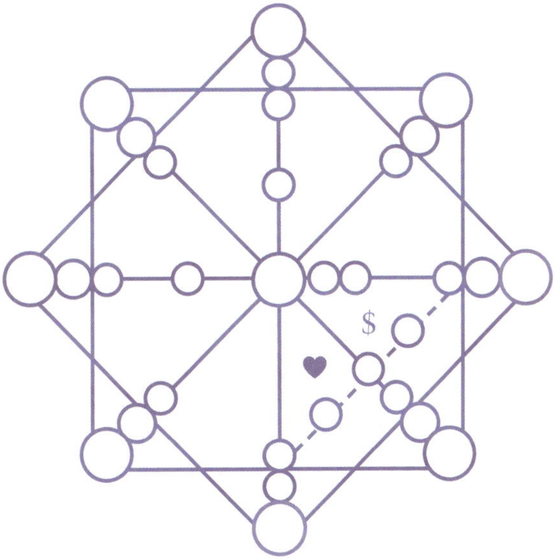

PART I

UNDERSTANDING YOUR DESTINY MATRIX

CHAPTER 1

THE STRUCTURE OF YOUR DESTINY MATRIX

HOW TO CALCULATE YOUR DESTINY MATRIX CHART

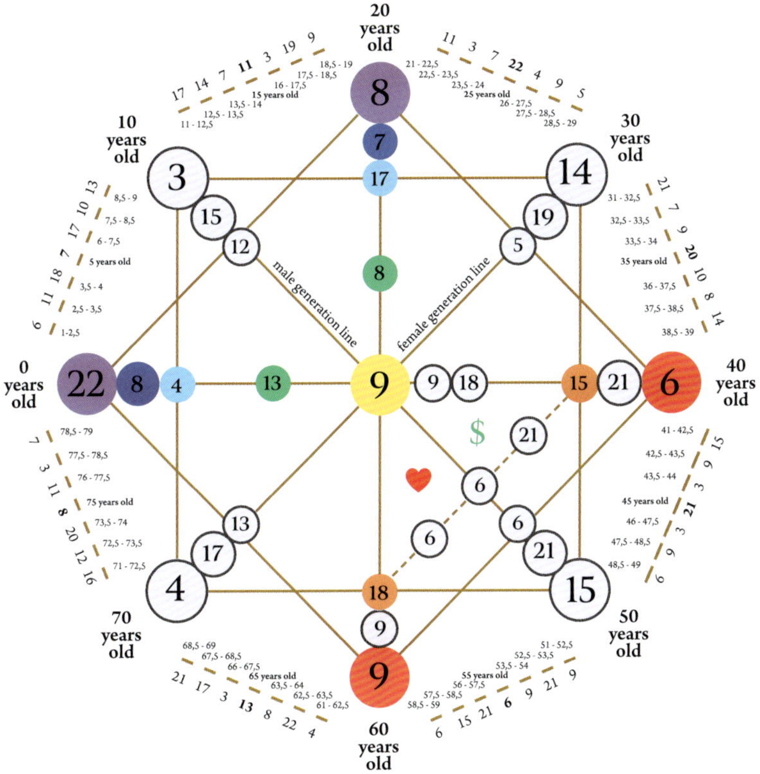

The chart shown above is an example for illustration purposes only and is based on my own birthday (22 August 1995). We have referred to this example chart throughout the book – all zoomed-in chart segments refer to the example above. Because the Destiny Matrix is calculated from your date of birth, each person's chart is unique, meaning your chart will contain a different combination of numbers.

To construct your chart manually, the next page contains a blank Destiny Matrix template containing letter codes that indicate specific calculations and positions within the chart. You can either draw this blank Destiny Matrix chart by hand or download an empty template from the internet and print it out. Then, simply follow the instructions provided on page 14 to fill in the numbers, starting with your birth date and going point by point with each calculation. Once completed, you can use your chart throughout this book to explore the meanings of each number and position within your personal matrix.

Creating Your Chart

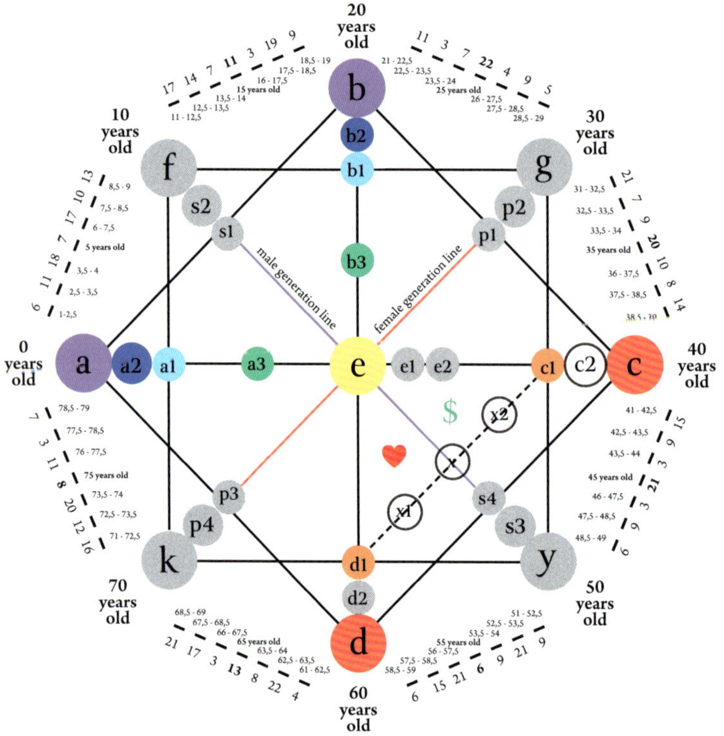

In the Destiny Matrix, numbers are meant to stay within the range of 1 to 22 because these correspond to the 22 Tarot's Major Arcana. If a calculation produces a number higher than 22, you must reduce it by adding its digits together until the result is 22 or less. For instance, 28 becomes 10, since 2 + 8 = 10. Likewise, the birth year 1995 becomes 6, since 1 + 9 + 9 + 5 = 24 and 2 + 4 = 6.

What Each Letter Means:

a = portrait zone = day of birth
b = connection to universe = month of birth
c = material tasks = year of birth
d = past life karma / karmic tasks = a + b + c
e = soul's comfort zone = a + b + c + d
a1 = experience with your kids = a + e
a2 = experience with your parents = a + a1
a3 = heart's wishes = a1 + e
b1 = past life talents = b + e
b2 = past life talents = b + b1
b3 = heart's wishes = b1 + e
c1 = prosperity blocks = c + e
c2 = material tasks = c + c1
d1 = love blocks = d + e
d2 = past life karma = d + d1
f = ancestral karma from father's side = a + b
g = ancestral karma from mother's side = b + c
y = ancestral karma from father's side = c + d
k = ancestral karma from mother's side = a + d
e1 = part of soul's comfort zone = f + g + y + k
e2 = part of soul's comfort zone = e + e1
s1 = ancestral karma from father's side = f + e1
s2 = ancestral karma from father's side = f + s1
p1 = ancestral karma from mother's side = g + e
p2 = ancestral karma from mother's side = g + p1
p3 = ancestral karma from mother's side = k + e
p4 = ancestral karma from mother's side = k + p3
s4 = ancestral karma from father's side = y + e
s3 = ancestral karma from father's side = y + s4
x = balance between love and finance = d1 + c1
x1 = your ideal partner = d1 + x
x2 = your ideal career = c1 + x

Creating Your Health Map

See page 112 for an explanation of your health map and its relationship to each chakra.

	Chakra name	Physics	Energy	Emotions
1	**Sahasrara** Mission	a	b	a+b
2	**Ajna** Destiny, egregores	a2	b2	a2+b2
3	**Vishuddha** Destiny, egregores	a1	b1	a1+b2
4	**Anahata** Relationships, picture of the world	a3	b3	a3+b3
5	**Manipura** Status, possessions	e	e	e+e
6	**Svadhisthana** Love of children, joy	c1	d1	c1+d1
7	**Muladhara** Body, *materia*	c	d	c+d
	Result Common energy	Physics: a+a2+a1+a3+e+c1+c=w Energy: b+b2+b1+b3+e+d1+d=z		w+z

Personal purpose:

Soul searching, balance of feminine and masculine qualities, abilities, skills

Sky: **b+d=(h)**
Earth: **a+c=(j)**
→ **h+j=(k)**

Personal for society and genus:

Tasks for genus, results and recognition in society

M: **f+y=(m)**
F: **g+k=(n)**
→ **m+n=(l)**

The letters 'M' and 'F' stand for 'Masculine' and 'Feminine' energies. They are calculated from the generational lines on the Destiny Matrix chart. In this calculation, F (Feminine) is derived from the female generation line by adding the two numbers at each end of that diagonal. M (Masculine) is derived from the male generation line in the same way; by adding the two numbers at each end.

General purpose for this lifetime:

Spiritual path, global task, where is the divine in me?

k+l=(o)

k = Personal purpose, l = Social purpose, o = Spiritual purpose

THE MATRIX BASICS

Just as each number and point in the Destiny Matrix carries meaning, the lines and shapes connecting them also hold significance. These structural elements form the framework of the chart and represent different energetic pathways within your life. Key features such as the octagram base, square shapes and various lines each correspond to specific themes and energetic influences. In the following pages, we will briefly explore what each of these elements represents within your Destiny Matrix.

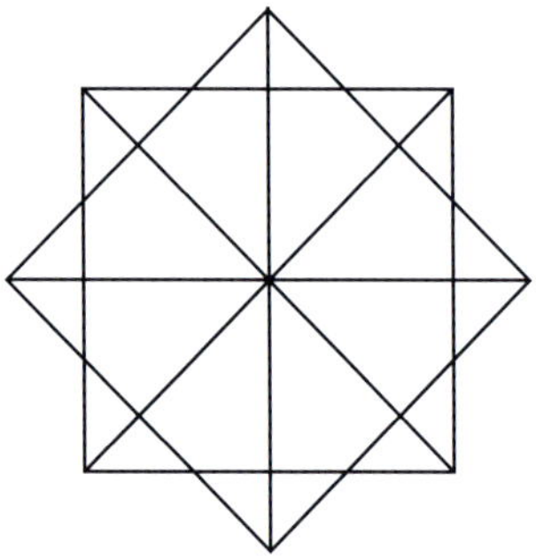

The Octagram

The Octagram

A square positioned straight and another placed diagonally on top of it form an octagram, an eight-pointed star. The octagram has had deep symbolic meaning across cultures throughout history, representing the unity of the spiritual and material worlds. It serves as a gateway to deeper perception, encouraging you to look beyond the physical realm and reflect on higher spiritual values.

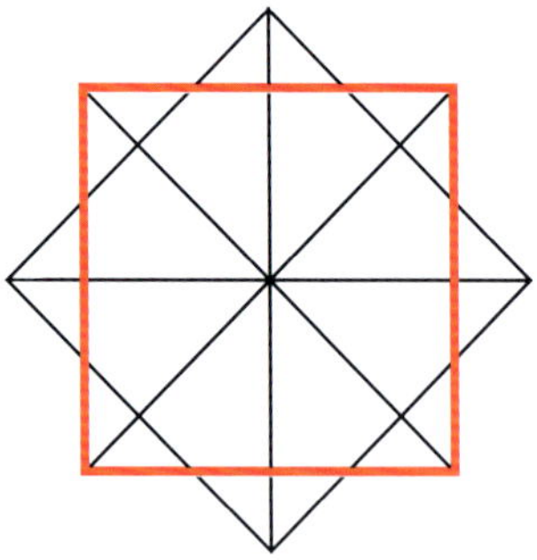

The Upright Square

The Upright Square

The upright square symbolizes your family ties, reflecting inherited tasks and skills and influences passed down through both paternal and maternal lines. Your family serves as the foundation of your identity; your personality and traits are shaped by your ancestors. So, the upright square reflects the fundamental qualities that guide you through life.

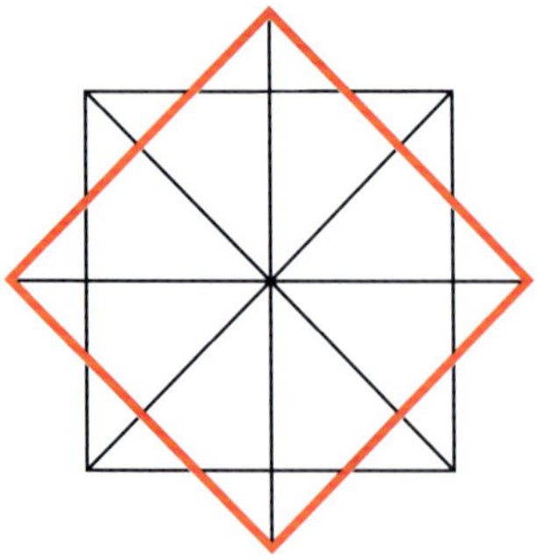

The Diagonal Square

The Diagonal Square

The diagonal square represents personal qualities connected to your soul, your unique energies within the Matrix, highlighting your strengths, talents, inner resilience, life lessons and personal growth journey.

The Sky Line

The vertical line extending from the upper corner to the lower corner of the octagram is known as the sky line. It represents your immaterial tasks – your journey of inner development and spiritual advancement.

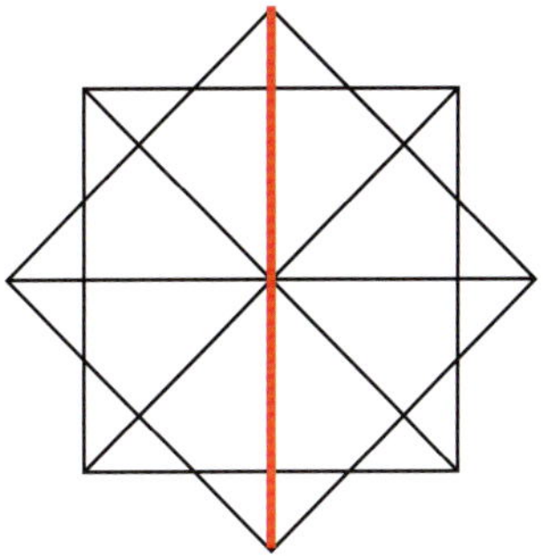

The Sky Line

The Earth Line

The horizontal line extending from the left corner to the right corner is called the Earth line. It symbolizes the material world, including all the aspects related to physical existence, such as money, health and tangible realities.

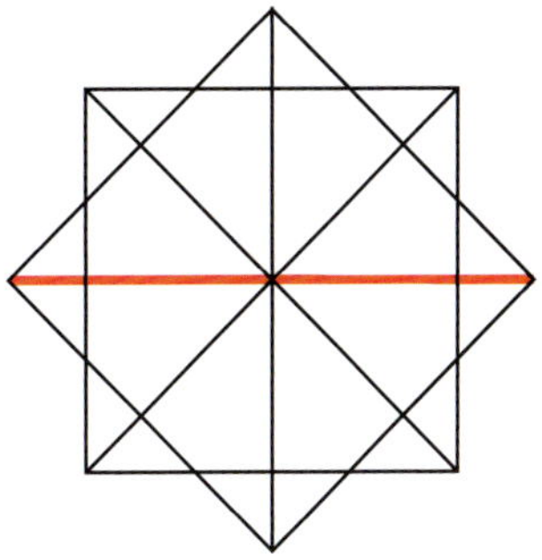

The Earth Line

Your Father's Lineage

The diagonal line extending from the upper left corner to the lower right corner, your male generation line, represents your father's lineage and the debts and gifts inherited from your paternal ancestors. This governs your societal fulfilment. It is also seen as the path of the inner masculine, reflecting your internal strength and personal development.

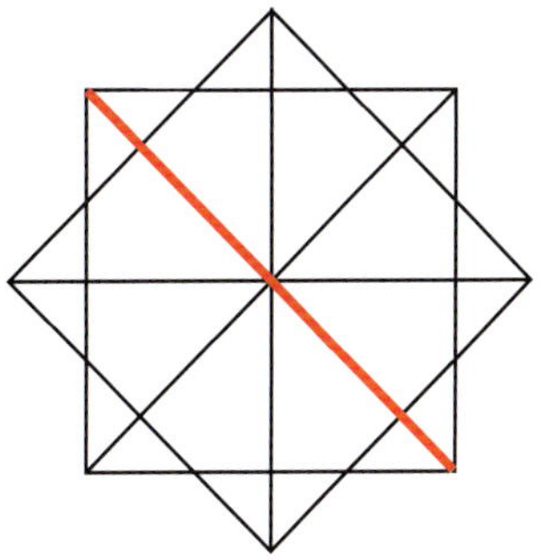

Your Father's Lineage

Your Mother's Lineage

The diagonal line extending from the upper right corner to the lower left corner, your female generation line, represents your mother's lineage and the debts and gifts inherited from your maternal ancestors. This influences your ability to build relationships. It is also seen as the path of the inner feminine, reflecting your emotional depth and nurturing qualities.

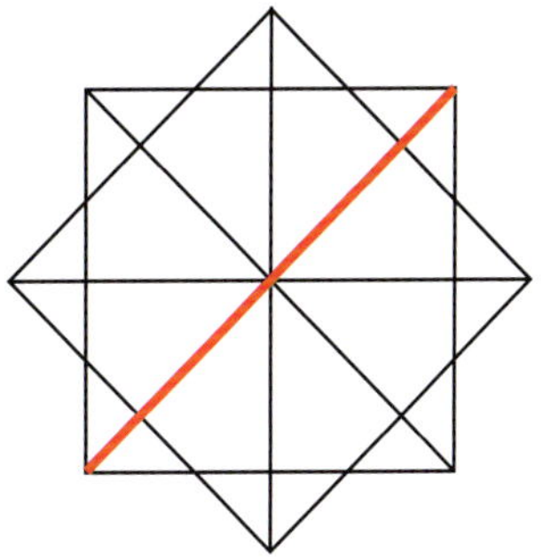

Your Mother's Lineage

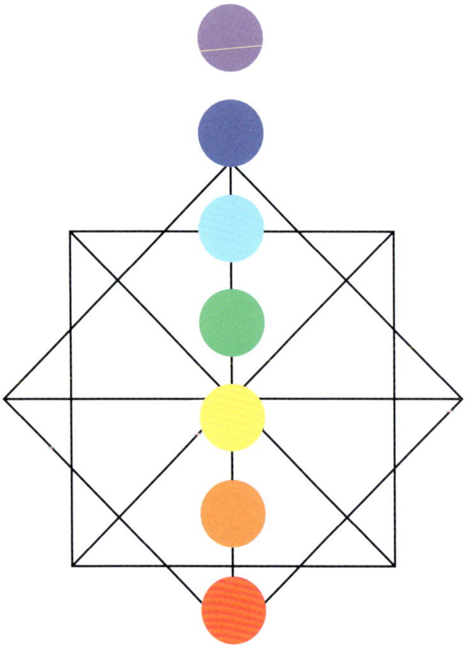

The Chakras and the Matrix

The Chakras and the Matrix

A chakra is a psycho-energetic centre within the human subtle body, an intersection of the channels through which *prana* (vital energy) flows. There are seven main chakras, governing physical, mental and emotional processes. The energies within the Matrix align with the chakra system, facilitating the understanding of specific zones.

Here are the chakras, from bottom to top:

Muladhara: The root chakra

The root chakra is connected to the material aspects of life, particularly fears related to safety and survival, which may arise when it is weak or unbalanced. When it is strong and balanced, you possess courage, resilience in the face of adversity and the ability to eliminate chaos and unfavourable situations from your life.

Svadhisthana: The sacral chakra

The sacral chakra is responsible for pleasure, creativity and sexuality. When it is weak or unbalanced, life may feel dull and lacking in joy, and sexual issues may arise. Conversely, when the sacral chakra is strong and balanced, you become more creative and able to fully enjoy life.

Manipura: The solar plexus chakra

The solar plexus chakra is the energy centre of willpower, ambition and personal strength. It is linked to your ability to set goals, as well as your energy, vitality and health. When it is weak or unbalanced, you may experience anger, resentment, depression and illness, and often lack clarity of purpose or understanding. You may also exhibit greed and harshness towards others. When it is strong and balanced, however, you are empowered, energetic and pursue your goals with confidence.

Anahata: The heart chakra

The heart chakra is the energy centre of love, compassion, patience, appreciation, gratitude and nobility. When it is weak or unbalanced, this may lead to negative emotions like hatred and envy, and a tendency to take without giving, only offering when it benefits yourself. If you have a blocked heart chakra, you will often prioritize others to your own detriment. However, when strong and balanced, this chakra fosters deep empathy and the ability to give and receive love freely.

Vishuddha: The throat chakra

The throat chakra is linked to your ability to communicate and express yourself truthfully. When it is weak or unbalanced, this can cause difficulties in expressing thoughts and emotions, even rudeness. Others may struggle to hear or understand your truth. However, when this chakra is strong and balanced, it greatly enhances your ability to communicate clearly and effectively.

Ajna: The third eye chakra

The third eye chakra governs learning, memory, intellect and attentiveness, intuition and the sixth sense. When it is weak or unbalanced, this can result in doubts, anxiety and confusion, causing you to limit your choices and be in the wrong place at the wrong time. Conversely, when it is strong and balanced, you become perceptive, intuitive and capable of making the right decisions, guided by inner wisdom and experience.

Sahasrara: The crown chakra

The crown chakra symbolizes cosmic consciousness and is considered the chakra of enlightenment. It represents your connection with your life purpose. When it is weak or unbalanced, this can lead to egocentrism, a limited perspective on reality and a weak connection with your soul. However, when it is strong and balanced, there is a deep union with your soul, fostering a sense of spiritual fulfilment and a clear connection to your higher purpose.

The Well-being Line

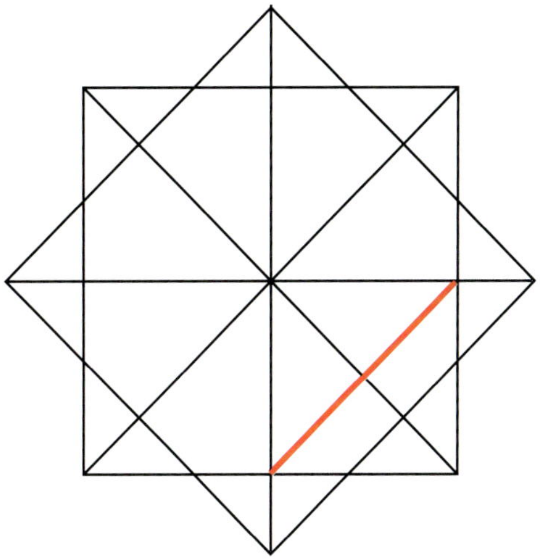

The Well-being Line

The well-being line corresponds to the second chakra (the sacral chakra) and governs the energies related to relationships and finances. It reflects the flow of material well-being and interpersonal connections.

CHAPTER 2

THE ARCANA OF DESTINY

THE 22 MAJOR ARCANA

As mentioned earlier, your Destiny Matrix is built on 22 universal energies, corresponding to the 22 Major Arcana of the Tarot. Each can be expressed in different ways, ranging from being challenging to promoting strength, wisdom and growth.

These energies are organized into three main realms:

- The World of Matter (energies 1–7): physical life, health, work, finances, social role and abundance.
- The World of Soul (energies 8–14): emotions, relationships and inner development.
- The World of Spirit (energies 15–21): spiritual awareness, higher understanding and consciousness.

Energy 22 represents transition, freedom and spiritual liberation.

Starting overleaf, we will look at the 22 Major Arcana in more detail.

THE 1ST ARCANA OF DESTINY

Associated with: The Magician

This represents personal power, creativity and the ability to express yourself in the world. It reflects new beginnings, self-awareness, leadership and the power of thought to shape reality. This energy supports growth, innovation and self-development, guiding you towards progress and creative realization.

When expressed negatively, it may appear as fear of change, lack of confidence or excessive ego, resistance to learning, loss of direction, negative thinking or the misuse of personal power in relationships and life choices.

THE 2ND ARCANA OF DESTINY

Associated with: The High Priestess

This represents unity, harmony and balance. It reflects connection with the universe, peace within familial and ancestral systems, and harmony between partners. This energy is linked to intuition, inner knowledge, reconciliation and the blending of opposites, such as masculine and feminine energies. It supports healing through relationships, emotional sensitivity and quiet inner wisdom.

In its negative expression, it may appear as inner conflict, indecision, emotional distance, fear of relationships, passivity, dishonesty or difficulty forming deep and stable connections.

THE 3RD ARCANA OF DESTINY

Associated with: The Empress

This represents fertility, motherhood and the feminine creative principle. It is connected to abundance, growth, care, family and the ability to create stability and prosperity in life. This energy supports nurturing, material well-being, home organization, social success and the healthy continuation of family lines. It can be expressed by everyone through creation, responsibility and material achievement.

In its negative form, it may appear as overcontrol within the family, fear for loved ones, family conflicts, lack of prosperity, difficulties related to motherhood or the female lineage, or an unhealthy attachment to power, career or control over children.

THE 4TH ARCANA OF DESTINY

Associated with: The Emperor

This represents power, authority, stability and material security. It reflects the masculine principle, leadership, responsibility, social status and the ability to create a strong foundation in life. This energy is connected to protection, structure, financial stability, ancestral strength and the preservation of ancient knowledge. Although associated with the masculine principle, it can be expressed by everyone.

In its negative form, it may appear as excessive control, rigidity, fear, financial difficulties, unhealthy attachment to power or material success, imbalance in family roles, lack of emotional rest, problems related to a paternal figure or ancestry and resistance to personal or spiritual growth.

THE 5TH ARCANA OF DESTINY

Associated with: The Hierophant

This represents law, order, knowledge and social structure. It reflects respect for traditions, family and national values, and the ability to learn, teach and pass on wisdom. This energy supports discipline, responsibility, mentorship and the creation and preservation of rules that organize society.

In its negative expression, it may appear as rigid control, the misuse of authority, excessive pride, resistance to learning, disrespect for elders or teachers, obsession with rules or the imposition of beliefs on others.

THE 6TH ARCANA OF DESTINY

Associated with: The Lovers

This represents love, relationships, beauty and emotional expression. It reflects the ability to give and receive love, create harmony in relationships and bring beauty into life through art, creativity and aesthetics. This energy supports openness of the heart, compassion, sensitivity, communication and self-expression in society.

In its negative form, it may appear as dependence on approval, focus on appearance over inner growth, emotional instability, unhealthy attachments, jealousy, lack of responsibility, the avoidance of personal growth or excesses in pleasure and lifestyle.

THE 7TH ARCANA OF DESTINY

Associated with: The Chariot

This represents movement, goals, leadership and victory. It reflects determination, competitiveness and the ability to lead others to shared success. This energy supports action, strategy, discipline, teamwork and steady progress towards meaningful goals.

In its negative expression, it may appear as lack of direction, passivity, doubt, aggression, the inability to complete tasks, poor focus, excessive pressure on others or an emphasis on material success without deeper purpose.

THE 8TH ARCANA OF DESTINY

Associated with: Justice

This represents justice, balance and the law of cause and effect. It reflects karmic principles, showing how actions, thoughts and choices return to you over time. This energy supports self-reflection, understanding past experiences and seeking inner truth rather than external judgement.

In its negative form, it may appear as inner imbalance, constant conflict, blaming others, excessive control, anxiety, depression or a strong sense that life and people are unfair.

THE 9TH ARCANA OF DESTINY

Associated with: The Hermit

This represents wisdom, depth and inner wholeness. It reflects healing on physical, emotional and spiritual levels, as well as a deep understanding of life and the interconnectedness of all beings. This energy supports self-sufficiency, compassion, conscious living, learning and healing through knowledge, words and experience.

In its negative expression, it may appear as isolation, emotional closure, physical or psychological imbalance, excessive seriousness, guilt, fear of intimacy or spiritual growth, and difficulty receiving appreciation or support from others.

THE 10TH ARCANA OF DESTINY

Associated with: The Wheel of Fortune

This represents life flow, intuition, luck and key turning-points. It reflects the ability to sense your true path and make choices that align with your personal destiny. This energy supports trust in life, timely opportunities, meaningful changes and conscious movement towards soul growth.

In its negative form, it may appear as weak intuition, confusion, lack of direction, dependence on others' opinions, the avoidance of responsibility, passivity or a feeling that life is heavy and unfocused.

THE 11TH ARCANA OF DESTINY

Associated with: Strength

This represents inner strength, passion, vitality and creative power. It reflects energy inherited from your ancestors, a strong life-force, inspiration and the ability to move ideas and people forwards. This energy supports leadership, focus, motivation and the confident expression of personal and creative potential.

In its negative expression, it may appear as aggression, excessive pressure on others, burnout, emotional outbursts, lack of balance, family conflicts, the misuse of power or the loss of connection with your roots and inner strength.

THE 12TH ARCANA OF DESTINY

Associated with: The Hanged Man

This represents service, compassion and seeing life from a higher perspective. It reflects a calling to help others, support family and society, and bring kindness and understanding into the world. This energy supports selfless care, spiritual awareness, creativity and meaningful contribution.

In its negative form, it may appear as excessive self-sacrifice, a lack of self-worth, emotional dependence, the inability to set boundaries, the avoidance of personal growth or a constant need to please others at the expense of yourself.

THE 13TH ARCANA OF DESTINY

Associated with: Death

This represents transformation, renewal and the start of new life cycles. It reflects the ability to let go of the old, complete what no longer serves and open space for change and growth. This energy supports rebirth, healing, creative renewal and adaptation to life's natural rhythms.

In its negative expression, it may appear as fear of change or loss, inner chaos, anxiety, excessive risk-taking, the inability to complete processes, emotional instability or resistance to personal and spiritual renewal.

THE 14TH ARCANA OF DESTINY

Associated with: Temperance

This represents a mature soul, strong intuition, joy and creative harmony with your true purpose. It supports spiritual growth, healing, creativity, connection with nature and guidance from dreams and higher forces.

In its negative expression, it may appear as disconnection from your soul, emotional instability, depression, aggression, materialism, blocked creativity, pride, control over others, jealousy, addictions and lack of spiritual growth.

THE 15TH ARCANA OF DESTINY

Associated with: The Devil

This represents power and engagement with the material world. It reflects influence, leadership, spiritual testing and the ability to manifest reality while maintaining integrity, free will and your connection to divine principles. This energy supports spiritual leadership, truth-seeing, unconditional love, the healing of addictions and the conscious use of power.

In its negative expression, it may appear as weak spiritual will, temptation, material obsession, greed, manipulation, the misuse of power, deception, egoism, addictions, distorted values, aggression and the loss of spiritual freedom.

THE 16TH ARCANA OF DESTINY

Associated with: The Tower

This represents awakening, revelation and radical transformation through the destruction of that which no longer serves a divine purpose. It reflects spiritual initiation, deep inner change, new insight and the rebuilding of life on a higher spiritual foundation. This energy supports spiritual leadership, clarity of purpose, faith, liberation from inner emptiness and conscious growth as a result of profound life changes.

In its negative expression, it may appear as aggression, resistance to change, fear, trauma, destructive behaviour or relationships, material fixation, unconscious actions, attachment to the past, addictions, ego dominance, chaos and the loss of spiritual direction.

THE 17TH ARCANA OF DESTINY

Associated with: The Star

This represents stellar energy, creativity, inspiration and the flow of divine talent from the Source. It reflects a strong connection to your true purpose, healing and intuitive abilities, artistic expression and the ability to inspire, unite and illuminate others through your personal gifts. This energy supports recognition, inner light, spiritual growth and the joyful sharing of talents with the world.

In its negative expression, it may appear as self-doubt, unrealized creativity, the loss of faith or vitality, emotional and mental imbalance, the judgement of others, pride or superiority, anxiety, conflict, spiritual disconnection and not expressing your true desires.

THE 18TH ARCANA OF DESTINY

Associated with: The Moon

This represents lunar energy, magnetism, intuition and personal magic. It reflects deep connection with the subconscious, clairvoyance, prophetic dreams, imagination and the ability to manifest through subtle perception and creative vision. This energy supports mysticism, rituals, artistic expression, conscious dreaming, aesthetics, inner depth and spiritual sensitivity.

In its negative expression, it may appear as fear, illusion, anxiety, spiritual stagnation, deception, addictions, emotional instability, the misuse or fear of inner power, material fixation, mental imbalance and disconnection from truth and higher awareness.

THE 19TH ARCANA OF DESTINY

Associated with: The Sun

This represents solar energy, light, leadership and an expansive influence for the benefit of many. It reflects service to society, creative self-expression, public activity and the ability to inspire, educate and unite people through personal radiance and vision. This energy supports leadership, large-scale projects, public speaking, recognition and sharing talents with the world.

In its negative expression, it may appear as egoism, the misuse of power, aggression, excessive control, materialism, a lack of spiritual values, emotional disconnection, pride, addiction, conflict, the suppression of others and the loss of gratitude and inner balance.

THE 20TH ARCANA OF DESTINY

Associated with: Judgement

This represents clarity, awakening and the bridge between the spiritual and material worlds. It reflects a deep connection with ancestral lineages, universal wisdom, intuition, prophecy and the ability to receive guidance through dreams, symbols and higher awareness. This energy supports spiritual awakening, the healing of ancestral karma, the integration of past and future, and conscious service as a conduit between heaven and Earth.

In its negative expression, it may appear as fear of inner abilities, disconnection from family and ancestry, pessimism, mental and emotional imbalance, addictions, spiritual stagnation, confusion, negative thinking and the loss of faith and clarity.

THE 21ST ARCANA OF DESTINY

Associated with: The World

This represents universal energy, expansion, unity and the completion of global cycles. It reflects service to humanity, peacemaking, large-scale creation and the ability to unite cultures, nations and beliefs through compassion and higher awareness. This energy supports global leadership, harmony, intuitive wisdom, connection with higher spiritual forces and the unconditional acceptance of life.

In its negative expression, it may appear as inner unrest, aggression, separation, fear of expansion or change, egoism, unresolved family conflicts, material domination, environmental harm, the inability to complete cycles and disconnection from universal values.

THE 22ND ARCANA OF DESTINY

Associated with: The Fool

This represents spiritual freedom, enlightenment and joyful liberation through Spirit. It reflects the highest level of spiritual evolution, lightness of being, creative revelation and the ability to live freely while guiding others to their true path. This energy supports ascension, spiritual communities, positive consciousness, travel, free expression and release from limitations and addictions.

In its negative expression, it may appear as inner blockages, lack of grounding, irresponsibility, fear of change, the misuse of freedom, unstable relationships, legal or authority issues, material or power dependence, mental imbalance and the loss of true inner freedom.

PART II

READING YOUR MATRIX

CHAPTER 3

YOUR PERSONAL QUALITIES

YOUR PORTRAIT ZONE

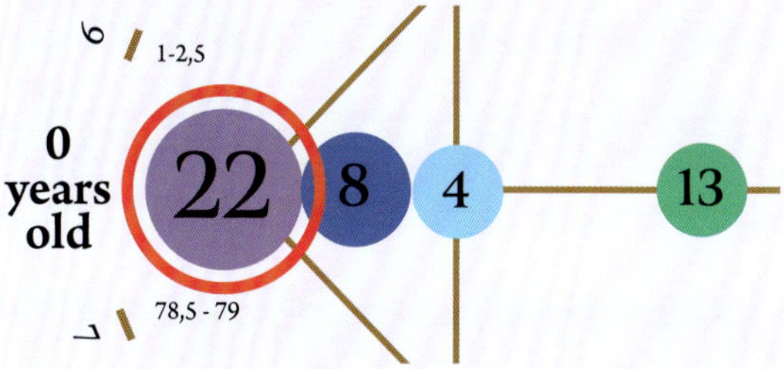

Your Portrait Zone

This is the energy tied to your birth number (the day you were born), representing the qualities you were born with and how these manifest in your life. It is the core energy that you carry throughout your life. It serves as your 'business card', offering a glimpse into your essence and shaping how others perceive you. It is crucial to live in alignment with this basic energy in a positive way, as your overall success and fulfilment are strongly influenced by how you embody it.

Note:
Due to the structure of the Destiny Matrix, not all interpretive sections begin with Arcana 1. Also, where the sections relate to the 12 months of the year, the sequence stops at 12. The masculine/feminine distinction is used only for Arcanas 3 and 4 due to their traditional titles (The Empress and The Emperor). No other Arcana in this system is gender-differentiated. If gendered language appears elsewhere in reference to other Arcana, it should be understood as neutral.

✷ ARCANA 1 ✷

You possess energy of a leader capable of shaping your own path and attracting followers through your unique ideas and confident self-expression. Your strengths are rooted in new beginnings, discovery and an instinctive understanding of life's hidden laws, allowing you to make transformative impacts. At your best, you radiate charisma, positivity and an adventurous spirit. However, misalignment brings challenges such as fear of change, ego inflation and self-doubt, leading to negativity and defensiveness. In your darker moments, you may isolate yourself or impose harsh standards on others while grappling with your own worthiness, revealing a more ruthless side that masks your powerful gifts.

✷ ARCANA 2 ✷

You embody a harmonious energy that seeks balance within yourself and in relationships, particularly between masculine and feminine energies. Your presence promotes peace and emotional clarity, and you possess an intuitive understanding of underlying emotions and connections. While you are diplomatic and influential in restoring harmony, disconnecting from this energy may lead to self-doubt, indecisiveness and emotional passiveness. This disconnection can manifest as avoiding commitment, hiding your true self or engaging in negative patterns such as laziness or seeking validation. Ultimately, your emotional state can become unstable when it drifts away from authenticity.

✷ ARCANA 3 ✷

You embody the qualities of growth, abundance and stability, and are adept at nurturing projects, relationships and material well-being. Your grounded presence fosters comfort and resource accumulation through responsibility and practical thinking, with a focus on long-term security. While you are often seen as kind and generous, challenges arise from a tendency to control, overprotect or become anxious about loved ones and outcomes. Family dynamics, particularly those linked to your maternal lineage, influence your fears and relationships. Feeling unappreciated can manifest, as can making demands and having your nurturing misunderstood as clinginess or dependence.

✷ ARCANA 4 ✷

You embody the energy of ancient structure and stability, drawing strength from your lineage and the wisdom of your ancestors. You navigate life with a sense of order and responsibility, and a capacity to build and protect both yourself and those around you. When aligned, this is evident in your respectable and grounded demeanour, logical thinking and disciplined actions. Challenges arise, however, when rigidity, control or the burdens of responsibility become overwhelming, leading to stress and emotional distance. You may find yourself overworking or struggling with expectations, while your need for structure might be misinterpreted as inflexibility or coldness.

✷ ARCANA 5 ✷

You embody the energy of structure, tradition and fundamental understanding. Your serious demeanour and authority lead others to view you as a knowledgeable guide. You excel at organizing information and maintaining order. While you may be perceived as strict yet fair, pitfalls include rigidity, imposing expectations and dismissing emotional insights. At your worst, you risk ignoring boundaries and misusing your knowledge, leading to perceptions of stubbornness. You are deeply rooted in traditions but may struggle with authority and sharing your insights.

✷ ARCANA 6 ✷

You express a vibrant love of life, people and beauty, and you naturally attract connection and warmth. Your artistry and emotional depth shine through in your communication and presentation, fostering relationships and social harmony. While your presence is compassionate and joyful, underlying challenges include perfectionism, emotional wounds and seeking validation. These can lead to clinginess, mood swings and struggles with boundaries, resulting in external perceptions of instability or drama. Your emotional sensitivity, although a strength, may sometimes manifest as inconsistency or irresponsibility in the eyes of others.

✷ ARCANA 7 ✷

You embody the essence of a dynamic leader and relentless achiever, characterized by agile energy, ambition and the ability to inspire others. Your life is action-oriented, filled with taking on new challenges. While you excel in uniting teams and executing complex strategies, your intense drive can manifest as aggression, envy or paranoia when misaligned. This intensity can also lead to difficulties in connection and moments of impatience or greed, clouding your ability to recognize your true desires.

✷ ARCANA 8 ✷

You possess a clear sense of justice and reason, observing the world through a logical lens. Your unwavering honesty and commitment are coupled with a strong inner critic, making you quick to identify faults in others and yourself. You see life in binary terms, often missing its full complexity, but the pursuit of karmic justice drives you to contemplate the deeper meanings of life events. While this can transform you and your surroundings positively, it may also result in frustration and anxiety when your expectations of fairness are unmet.

✷ ARCANA 9 ✷

You possess philosophical depth, approaching life with thoughtful insight. Your introverted nature thrives in solitude, which brings you clarity and energetic restoration, while noise and crowds unsettle you. You are guided by intuition and you understand life's interconnectedness. While you provide healing to others through your sincerity, your depth can lead to self-doubt and harsh judgements of both yourself and others. You seek connection, yet often hesitate to trust, clinging to past memories and lessons. Your journey involves healing yourself to heal others and finding a balance between your emotional depth and a more open-hearted approach to life.

✷ ARCANA 10 ✷

You possess a natural ease in navigating life, often guided by fortune, which results in a cheerful and approachable demeanour. Your adaptability allows new experiences to flow effortlessly and this is aided by your intuition. However, disconnection from this inner guidance can lead to passivity and a drift from your true path, characterized by procrastination and external influences. True alignment is achieved through taking responsibility for your journey and utilizing your intuition to create a meaningful and dynamic life.

✷ ARCANA 11 ✷

You carry the power of your ancestors, a flame that drives you on with intensity and vigour. Your presence inspires those around you. Nevertheless, while you possess the ability to lead and create and can embody strength and courage, your energy can lead to burnout or conflicts if unbalanced. You may struggle with arrogance and judging others harshly, as well as experience exhaustion and disconnection. Your nature allows for both creation and chaos, underscoring the importance of channelling your power effectively.

✷ ARCANA 12 ✷

You are a compassionate individual driven by a deep instinct to help others, often prioritizing their needs over your own. Your gentle presence and intuitive nature allow you to easily connect on an emotional level, bringing healing and understanding. However, this selflessness can lead to burnout and self-sacrifice, and you may feel overwhelmed or lost. You possess the ability to see new possibilities and connect with deeper meanings in life, yet you may find yourself trapped in unbalanced relationships that leave you feeling empty.

✷ ARCANA 13 ✷

You possess a wandering mind that seeks deeper meaning and unconventional answers, driven by intense emotions and a curiosity about technology and innovation. But, while you look to the future, you can also be burdened by memories and grief, which can clutter your emotional and physical space. You are at a crossroads of endings and beginnings, experiencing the tension of renewal amid a fear of change. You feel the cycles of life, death and rebirth, and may worry about loved ones and ageing, even though understanding these themes is part of your journey. When you align with your positive energy, you can restore and reinvent yourself and the world; however, resistance to change can cloud your path. Nonetheless, you possess the power to release what no longer serves you and evolve into a wiser self.

✷ ARCANA 14 ✷

You possess a quiet modesty and natural tact that creates a calming presence, and with your patience and grounded nature, you embody a deep inner worth and maturity. Your impeccable manners and simple yet tasteful style reflect your creative, artistic soul, aligning with your energetic links to water and inspiration. You can channel insights through dreams and connect with nature, enhancing the harmony of your surroundings. However, disconnecting from this inner harmony and neglecting spiritual development may lead to impatience, aggression, emotional instability, pride or even addictions.

✷ ARCANA 15 ✷

You possess magnetic charisma that attracts attention, coupled with a profound understanding of human nature. You exude luxury and a love of intense experiences, yet you can sometimes exhibit manipulative tendencies. Your journey challenges your spiritual strength and urges you to grow beyond mere impulse and the manifestation of earthly pleasures. With innate leadership qualities, you have the potential to guide others, advocating for freedom and unconditional love. However, disconnection from your inner strength may lead to indulgence in excess, self-serving behaviours and struggles with willpower. Challenges on your journey include maintaining spiritual clarity and controlling cravings for power and material comfort.

✷ ARCANA 16 ✷

You possess a dynamic and intense energy that both captivates and intimidates others, yet you embody resilience, having endured challenges that have rendered you fearless and transformative. Your energy signifies change, often the dismantling of the obsolete to make way for new beginnings. Although you will face significant trials, each will contribute to your spiritual growth and understanding of existence. You can inspire awakening in others, yet when disconnected from your core, your fierce nature may lead to destructiveness, defensiveness and impulsiveness, as you can struggle with fear and attachment to the past.

✷ ARCANA 17 ✷

You embody a quiet nobility with an aristocratic charm and a compassionate heart. Your commitment to your endeavours showcases precision and mastery, illuminated by a luminous energy that seeks beauty, purity and purpose. This deep connection to a creative and healing flow allows you to channel inspiration, drawing people to you and inspiring unity and admiration. However, a loss of confidence or disconnection from your purpose can lead to pessimism and stagnation, risking the burial of your talents amid a dull routine. Then, your sensitivity may shift to anxiety, and pride can become superiority, causing a withdrawal from creative expression and a dimming of your inner light.

✷ ARCANA 18 ✷

You possess a mystical and creative soul, characterized by intuition and ancient wisdom. Your imagination is potent, allowing you to perceive unseen energies and phenomena. Tied to lunar cycles, you exhibit traits of clairvoyance and a talent for ritual magic and manifesting desires. This energy enables you to create beauty and meaning while also granting you philosophical insights. However, it can also lead to emotional turmoil, anxiety and depressive moods, particularly when your energy is unsettled. In these moments, you may struggle with self-doubt and retreat into harmful habits, disconnecting from your creativity and spiritual path.

✷ ARCANA 19 ✷

You possess a radiant and generous personality, exuding positivity and strength that inspire others. Your magnetic energy and leadership qualities naturally draw people to you, making you a catalyst for growth and transformation. While you thrive in public and creative roles, your intense emotions can create challenges, leading to tendencies towards moodiness, pride and possessiveness when you are feeling insecure. It's important to remain connected to gratitude and humility to prevent your inner light from overshadowing those around you.

✷ ARCANA 20 ✷

You embody a voice that resonates with ideas, beliefs and projects, advocating for truth and defending your home and loved ones with deep loyalty and strong family values. Balancing between spiritual and earthly realms, you carry ancestral wisdom and insights that allow you to heal and unite. Despite this, however, you may struggle with harsh judgements and fears, leading to moments of withdrawal or confusion. Your spiritual abilities can create inner conflict and emotional weight when overwhelmed by the expectations tied to your lineage.

✷ ARCANA 21 ✷

You are a wise and respected individual who embodies compassion and diplomacy, with a global perspective focused on humanity. Your energy is one of healing and building, guided by protective feminine energies and spiritual wisdom. Equipped with an intuitive understanding of what unites people across cultures and conflicts, you seek to create peace and harmony, yet your idealism may lead to frustration, irritability and a disconnection from your spiritual centre when your ideals are not reflected in the world around you.

✷ ARCANA 22 ✷

You possess a vibrant and uplifting spirit, characterized by cheerfulness, humour and childlike openness, which instantly brightens any room. You pursue growth and new experiences, thriving when connected to like-minded individuals. Your energy fosters movement and exploration, inspiring others while embodying joy and freedom. However, your impulsiveness may lead to recklessness and pose challenges in maintaining stability and long-term commitments, making you susceptible to escapism and a lack of direction at times. Your quest for freedom can also result in shallow connections and misunderstandings when you're detached from your deeper purpose.

YOUR SOUL'S COMFORT ZONE

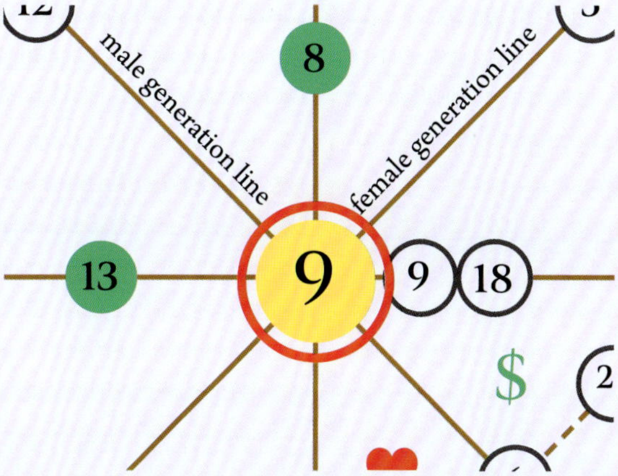

Your Soul's Comfort Zone

Your soul's comfort zone is a resource energy, a deep internal force. It is the state in which you feel fully energized and at peace, and the state your soul strives for, as it brings the greatest harmony and balance. In this state, you are aligned with your true essence and experience a profound sense of inner fulfilment.

✷ ARCANA 3 ✷

You find fulfilment in creation and nurturing, flourishing when you care for others and express yourself artistically. Your need to share your talents stems from a desire for community connection, and you radiate emotional intelligence and generosity. You thrive when respected and appreciate pleasant interactions. Embracing support enhances your well-being, while learning to delegate helps to avoid overwhelm, and a focus on beauty and abundance reflects your worth. Comfort comes from nurturing ideas and creating harmonious environments, and your energy promotes balance and grounded abundance.

✷ ARCANA 4 ✷

You thrive in stability and structure, finding comfort in a well-organized life where career, finances and personal goals advance purposefully. Achieving financial independence and creating something of your own will provide you with both material security and fulfilment. You excel when planning clearly and maintaining your physical health through discipline and routine. Your ideal environment is an orderly and professional one, where respect and recognition are paramount, and you naturally attract leadership roles. Balancing ambition with meaningful connections enhances your confidence. Socially, you flourish in responsible company and through accepting support.

✷ ARCANA 5 ✷

You evolve through steady learning, with your family as the root system that shapes your values and provides stability. For you, fairness, integrity and lawful behaviour are the essential principles that foster trust and respect. As you grow spiritually and mentally, you gain the clarity to guide others and embrace acceptance and compassion in relationships. This leads to calm confidence and respect for natural hierarchies. Your effectiveness as a communicator and mentor increases when you speak from vulnerability and experience. Fulfilment comes from learning, teaching and engaging in meaningful practices, strengthened by harmony at home and community connections.

✷ ARCANA 6 ✷

You thrive in balanced partnerships focused on sharing financial goals, enhancing trust and strengthening relationships. Then, harmony extends beyond money to health and well-being, creating a fulfilling life encompassing work, rest, leisure and connection. You value sincere relationships akin to family, embracing the beauty and complexity of life. With a natural sense of joy, you promote acceptance and gratitude, facilitating harmonious interactions. Your fulfilment stems from personal achievements rather than external validation, leading to deeper emotional connections and mutual support.

✷ ARCANA 7 ✷

Your soul thrives on motion, variety and freedom. You grow by enjoying the journey to your goals, as movement and sports foster discipline, resilience and focus. Shared goals strengthen relationships and, when you are active and purposeful, both inner harmony and outer success will follow. Stagnation is detrimental and you struggle in rigid environments, but flourish with companions who align with your own pace. Dynamic activities, goal-setting and tracking achievements energize you, while rest and meditation maintain balance. You are comfortable embracing challenges and new experiences and inspiring others with your resilience and optimism.

✷ ARCANA 8 ✷

You are at ease when developing through knowledge and education, which will enable decision-making and leadership in complex processes. Honesty and fairness guide your career growth, fostering trust within teams. You seek balance and understanding, acting as a mediator and valuing clarity and structure. Analysing cause and effect deepens your insight, while recognition and community involvement enhance your inner harmony. Engaging with diverse cultures and esoteric knowledge strengthens your grounded essence.

✷ ARCANA 9 ✷

You flourish when searching out and connecting with like-minded people, exchanging knowledge that broadens your horizons. Meaningful conversations and healthcare practices clear your mind, allowing for deep relationships that enhance mutual understanding. Your evolution involves understanding yourself, healing and uniting the spiritual and material aspects of life. You embody wisdom and depth, serving as a healer and philosopher. You find comfort in solitude and one-on-one connections, drawing power from silence and nature. Observing patterns and treating solitude as nourishment contribute to the quality of your life, along with good food and thoughtful habits.

✷ ARCANA 10 ✷

You thrive and grow by putting trust in your intuition and embracing change. By following your inspirations, you enhance the quality of your endeavours and call forwards dynamic, supportive relationships. Evolution comes from breaking free of external influences and learning to act with clarity and confidence. You embody freedom and insight, finding comfort in movement and meaningful connections, while also valuing solitude and mindfulness practices. You balance spiritual and physical well-being, aligning with the flow and honouring your intuition, which attracts others to your calming and wise energy.

✷ ARCANA 11 ✷

You flourish by learning to relax and channel your energy towards creativity and connection. Helping others unlock their potential enhances your own well-being, and the open expression of your feelings strengthens your relationships. You maintain balance through surrounding yourself with positivity, along with self-love, rest, meditation and nature. Engaging in movement and shared projects energizes you and uplifts others through your compassion and diplomacy. You find comfort in applying your willpower to daily tasks, celebrating small achievements while cultivating resilience and joy. Conflicts become opportunities for awareness and growth, teaching patience and understanding.

✷ ARCANA 12 ✷

You thrive by establishing personal boundaries, valuing your work and trusting your intuition, which fosters both trust and rapport with others while safeguarding your emotional well-being. To enhance creativity and reduce stress, you engage in music, meditation and movement, alongside reflection and silence for self-discovery. Balancing kindness towards others with self-care, you recognize your worth and maintain humility and equality in interactions. Your soul flourishes in connection with nature and personal space, where you can find comfort and reflection as you continuously expand your consciousness and embrace new perspectives.

✷ ARCANA 13 ✷

You grow through adaptability and courage, transforming life's changes into opportunities for growth. Challenges strengthen you, and you thrive by remaining flexible in work and in relationships, valuing partnerships built on mutual respect and shared experiences. You facilitate change, releasing outdated beliefs while retaining wisdom, and attract others with your depth and patience. Your soul seeks novelty, and you recharge through nature and movement, consciously shifting routines to keep life stimulating. Embracing freedom and clearing clutter sustain your creativity and focus.

✷ ARCANA 14 ✷

You thrive by cultivating patience, balance and harmony within yourself and your environment. You realize true wealth lies in moderation across finances, food, work and leisure. You foster heartfelt relationships and your soul flourishes in joy and gratitude, as you learn to release burdens like resentment and judgement. Meditation and communion with nature restore your energy and bring comfort, while art and music inspire you. As a healer and guide, you teach the appreciation of beauty and balance, creating a harmonious home and enriching your life through creativity and cultural experiences. You attune to life's rhythms, embracing grace in everyday moments and transforming daily tasks into a meditative journey to soulful mastery.

✷ ARCANA 15 ✷

You evolve through mindfulness, discipline and self-awareness, which are crucial for overcoming unhealthy habits. Engaging in regular physical activity enhances your willpower and resilience, enabling you to resist temptations. A life enriched with passion and creativity fosters joy and openness to change, leading to a fulfilling existence. Your experiences grant you wisdom and compassion, allowing you to support others through their struggles. By embodying mastery and leadership, you promote joy, creativity and self-expression. Developing your self-confidence and influence helps you to channel desires into meaningful goals, inspiring and empowering others to transform their lives too.

✷ ARCANA 16 ✷

You thrive through reassessing your beliefs and embracing change, viewing challenges as catalysts for growth. A focus on self-reflection and spiritual alignment will guide you to a life led by clarity and higher consciousness. This journey involves merging the spiritual and material realms and positioning yourself as a leader and guide. Inner balance is maintained through mindfulness, forgiveness and helping others overcome limiting beliefs. Emphasizing conscious adaptation fosters resilience and clarity, while creating a sanctuary of simplicity and peace at home satisfies your personal needs.

✷ ARCANA 17 ✷

Empathy and creativity are pivotal in shaping your life, enabling a deep understanding of others and self-expression through various forms of art. This serves as a conduit for hope and healing. By transcending ego and fear, you become a healing and transformative presence, fostering connection and recognition. You thrive on engaging in practices that maintain clarity and inspire others, nurturing their potential. Your journey involves immersing yourself in beauty and symbolism, experiencing the world as a rich tapestry of emotions and inspiration.

✷ ARCANA 18 ✷

For you, comfort is found in holistic self-care, which encompasses body care, emotional well-being and mental practices like relaxation and meditation. Growth requires facing fears as well as dismantling inner blocks, but embracing new experiences fosters confidence and creativity. A blend of psychological awareness and curiosity will form a foundation for a fulfilling life, and with a clear perception of reality and connection to higher powers, you can harness your intuitive gifts for transformation and manifestation. Positive thinking and intention-setting will also help you to flourish. You have a preference for intimate connections, creativity through intuitive art and a nurturing home environment. It is vital for you to honour emotional cycles and create a sacred, soothing space filled with warmth and beauty.

✷ ARCANA 19 ✷

For you, a fulfilled life is built on physical vitality, joy and social openness. Maintaining your health through movement, nutrition and rest gives you the energy for active participation in society. Emotional well-being is nurtured through joy, laughter and connections with loved ones, particularly children, fostering empathy and kindness. Exuding confidence and warmth, you are a natural leader capable of influencing various fields. Your engagement in public life, along with a focus on community and service, aligns with your purpose and is fuelled by gratitude. Embracing creativity and maintaining a joyful spirit while managing ambitious goals will ensure sustainable growth without burnout.

✷ ARCANA 20 ✷

You initiate growth by reviewing your personal values and fostering inner harmony. Your emotional and spiritual well-being is crucial for a balanced life and is supported by practices like meditation and yoga, which facilitate true self-awareness. In turn, this clarity promotes peace, confidence and a personal journey. A spiritual awakening will alter ancestral karma, allowing you to combine maternal and paternal energies and unlock the potential to act as a healer and mentor. By channelling higher energies, you can find purpose in everyday life and encourage others through insight and gentle persuasion. Maintaining a positive and communicative approach, particularly in familial relationships, helps dissolve inherited fears and grievances, promoting authentic living. Family support, enhanced through shared traditions and stories, deepens belonging and reveals ancestral wisdom, providing you with the stability and strength for a prosperous future.

✷ ARCANA 21 ✷

Openness and travel are your keys to growth and self-realization. Engaging with diverse cultures will enhance your understanding and foster universal human values. Careers involving travel and cross-cultural collaboration are particularly rewarding for you, providing creative, socially conscious work while promoting harmony, freedom and prosperity. By cultivating tolerance and expanding consciousness, you not only flourish personally but also contribute to the well-being of humanity and the Earth.

✷ ARCANA 22 ✷

True fulfilment arises for you from valuing the intangible aspects of life such as love, friendship and personal growth while maintaining a balanced relationship with material possessions. Flexibility and freedom from attachment enhance your adaptability, while engaging in new experiences, challenges and creative endeavours promotes personal development and harmony. Your journey entails cultivating inner freedom, nurturing positive ancestral karma and joyfully pursuing new projects. Additionally, prioritizing physical and emotional well-being, connecting with nature and embracing artistic expression bring you comfort. Genuine communication and connections encourage spiritual growth, while releasing rigid beliefs and negative emotions keeps your energy light.

YOUR HEART'S WISHES

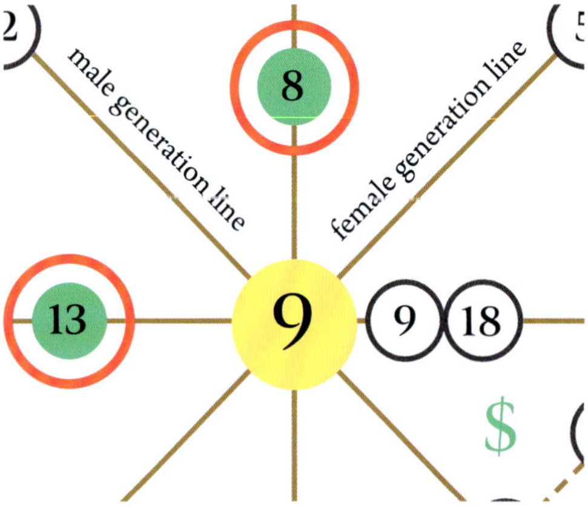

Your Heart's Wishes

✷ ARCANA 3 ✷

At heart, you desire a grounded, nurturing life centred on home, family and emotional closeness. You seek harmony in your household, deep bonds with your loved ones, shared meals and meaningful daily traditions. You feel fulfilled when you create comfort, care for nature and build or lead meaningful work. Giving to others through nourishment, practical care and kindness brings you joy and a steady inner strength that allows love and self-expression to flow naturally.

✷ ARCANA 4 ✷

At heart, you desire a life of strength, purpose and steady creation. You are drawn to leadership, clear action and tangible results: building a home, growing a business and providing security for those you love. Family unity, shared meals and the role of protector and guide deeply fulfil you. You value generosity, craftsmanship and restoring life through building, gardening and care. Honouring these qualities gives you confidence and direction.

✷ ARCANA 5 ✷

At heart, you desire clarity, wisdom and inner order. You are fulfilled by healing, learning and sharing knowledge, by bringing life, documents and family systems into order and harmony. A deep connection with nature, ancestral land and family traditions nourishes you, as do gatherings with relatives and like-minded spiritual people. You feel called to grow through spiritual work, guidance from teachers and working through ancestral wisdom and karma. Teaching, public speaking, consulting and caring for loved ones and animals bring you joy and purpose.

✷ ARCANA 6 ✷

At heart, you desire unconditional love, both for yourself and others. You feel fulfilled when you give attention, offer kind words and thoughtful gifts and create beauty in how you look and in the spaces you live in. Romance, heartfelt conversations with your partner and warm connections with family and friends nourish you deeply. You are energized by social gatherings, celebrations and bringing people together through joyful events.

✷ ARCANA 7 ✷

At heart, you desire progress, victory and forward movement. You are energized by setting goals, shaping your path and taking decisive action. Travel, physical activity and dynamic pursuits make you feel alive, while leading, organizing and training others gives you purpose. You feel fulfilled when you gather a team around your vision and inspire people to move together towards a shared goal.

✷ ARCANA 8 ✷

At heart, you desire truth, meaning and a deep understanding of life's order. You are inspired by seeing cause and effect clearly and accepting reality as it is, trusting that everything is fair. Philosophical conversations, meditation and spiritual practices bring you peace and insight. You are nourished by art, music, meaningful films and the wisdom found in books, psychology and karmic knowledge. Nature, sacred places, ancient artefacts, early mornings and a steady daily rhythm ground you.

✷ ARCANA 9 ✷

At heart, you desire silence, depth and inner strength. You are inspired when life slows down and you are alone with yourself and nature in reflection, study and healing work. Meaningful books, thoughtful films, meditation, disciplined spiritual practices and writing down your insights all nourish you deeply. You value resilience, clarity and the ability to rise above temptation. Connections with spiritually aligned friends and healing or counselling work feel natural and fulfilling to you.

✷ ARCANA 10 ✷

At heart, you desire ease, trust and gentle guidance from life and the Divine. You are inspired when you relax into faith, noticing signs along your path and feeling supported by higher forces. Moving with the flow, sharing experiences with friends and working within a team feel natural to you. Group practices, journeys and self-development seminars nourish your spirit, as does exploring your destiny through numerology and guidance work. Nature walks, meditation, harmonious art and travelling the world fill you with light and meaning.

✷ ARCANA 11 ✷

At heart, you desire joy, passion and creative expression. You are inspired when you engage in work you love, share love and intimacy and explore your own self-discovery. Time in nature, helping and connecting with family and celebrating together around a warm table bring you fulfilment. Outdoor work, hikes to powerful places and active leisure energize your spirit.

✷ ARCANA 12 ✷

At heart, you desire to give, serve and share your energy with others. You are inspired by helping your loved ones, connecting at warm family gatherings and offering healing or guidance. Communion with nature, the elements and the Divine fills you with a sense of peace, as do travel and spiritual practices that align you with higher vibrations. Learning, self-discovery and sharing wisdom with like-minded friends and spiritual communities nourish your soul.

✷ ARCANA 13 ✷

At heart, you desire change, adventure and renewal. You are inspired by new experiences, travel and transforming your surroundings. Active recreation, gardening, building and furnishing your home and working with the Earth bring you joy. You are drawn to uncovering the past: exploring ancient sites, studying fate and karma, and giving old things new life. Hiking, climbing and embracing life's extremes energize you.

✷ ARCANA 14 ✷

At heart, you desire joy, harmony and a lightness of being. You are inspired by heartfelt connections, warm conversations and gatherings with kindred spirits. Nature, water and the guidance of angels bring you peace and inspiration. Art, spiritual and psychological practices and mindful moderation nourish your soul. You feel fulfilled by a cosy home life, harmony with your loved ones and caring for both body and emotions through cleansing and balance.

✷ ARCANA 15 ✷

At heart, you desire intensity, power and deep experience. You are inspired by what is magnetic, forbidden and transformative, seeking both pleasure and control in equal measure. Exploring your desires, confronting your shadows and turning inner struggles into strength bring you fulfilment. Mastering temptation, building influence and channelling passion into purpose empower your path. Emotional depth, sensual connection, balance between light and darkness, ancestral connection, travel to sacred places and the energy of nature awaken your spirit.

✷ ARCANA 16 ✷

At heart, you desire presence, insight and connection with the Divine. You are inspired by feeling the sacred in every moment, receiving inner revelations and deepening your spiritual practice through meditation and self-discovery. Travel, movement, creativity and active leisure awaken your spirit, as do retreats, training and guiding others on their spiritual path. You feel fulfilled by leading, mentoring and transforming both your inner and outer worlds through restructuring and change.

✷ ARCANA 17 ✷

At heart, you desire unity with the Divine and the joy of co-creating with it. You are inspired by radiant energy, creative expression and bringing goodness to your family, humanity and the Earth. Music, art, healing and consulting work fill you with purpose, as do meditation and connections with spiritual companions. Nature, the elements, the sky, stars, mountains, gardens and the care of plants and pets awaken your spirit.

✷ ARCANA 18 ✷

At heart, you desire to understand life's hidden energies and the mysteries of the world. You are inspired by rituals, miracles and the magic of the universe. The starry sky, the moon, sacred places, oceans and nature awaken your soul. Meditation, spiritual practices and caring for both body and soul bring you clarity and strength. Art, creativity, philosophy, healing and esoteric practices fill you with purpose, as do writing, divination and crafting beauty in all its forms.

✷ ARCANA 19 ✷

At heart, you desire light, purpose and meaningful connection. You are inspired by the sunrise, the energy of the sun and the element of fire. Creating, sharing knowledge and serving others through social projects, leadership and public speaking bring you fulfilment. You feel alive in nature, among spiritual companions and with like-minded people pursuing a common goal. Travelling, organizing events, running your own business and uniting art, society and spirituality nourish your spirit.

✷ ARCANA 20 ✷

At heart, you desire connection, wisdom and the flow of divine knowledge. You are inspired by meditation, prayer, energy work and unity with higher forces. Helping and healing your family, loved ones and others fills your soul, as do heartfelt communication and shared moments at the family table. Working with your ancestral lineage, practising ancestral healing and connecting with ancestral lands and nature awaken your spirit. Spiritual and physical purification, fasting and sharing wisdom with others bring you purpose and fulfilment.

✷ ARCANA 21 ✷

At heart, you desire peace, service and harmony with the world. You are inspired by acts of goodness, creative projects and the expansion of meaningful work. Travel and connection with the loving universe awaken your spirit. Meditation, spiritual initiation, fasting and purification nourish your soul, as do sharing healing knowledge and serving both your family and humanity. Nature, the elements and the energy of Mother Earth give you strength and inspiration.

✷ ARCANA 22 ✷

At heart, you desire freedom, connection and expansive experiences. You are inspired by the liberty to choose, create and act, and by the vastness of the world and all its people. Travel, sacred places, mountains and nature awaken your spirit, while new projects and creative endeavours fill you with purpose. Meditation, fasting, prayer and spiritual purification strengthen you, as do sharing healing knowledge and guiding others in their destiny. Family harmony, ancestral work, large-scale events, festivals and spiritual leadership bring you fulfilment.

CHAPTER 4

YOUR FAMILY RELATIONSHIPS

YOUR EXPERIENCE WITH YOUR PARENTS

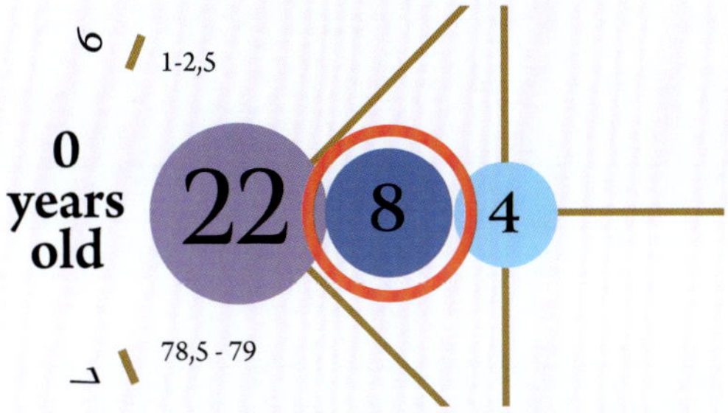

Your Experience With Your Parents

✷ ARCANA 2 ✷

Growing up, mixed signals around you made truth hard to read. Rules applied to you, but not to them. That left you confused, so you learned to please, stay quiet and hide what you really felt. With time, being 'easy' for others became normal for you. Healing begins when you start to trust your own senses and open up to support instead of pretending everything is fine. Then, your real emotions come to the fore, your voice strengthens and honesty feels safer. As you listen to your inner signals, intuition and body, life slowly becomes brighter and more alive.

✷ ARCANA 3 ✷

Early life may have been shaped by a dominant caregiving figure who carried burdens alone, struggled with trust or imposed strong control. Adulthood may bring you difficulty accepting emotional closeness, to the point of rejecting caregiving roles yourself. Healing begins with recognizing their limitations and choosing compassion over resentment. Learn to share responsibility, ask for support, soften control and build trust. Growth comes through restoring inner authority and directing your drive towards purposeful, constructive action. In balance, this energy becomes creative, nurturing and responsibly powerful: able to care for others without self-sacrifice, to lead without domination and to act with fairness and accountability. It unites strength with tenderness, giving with receiving and allows fulfilment through relationships, meaningful work, creativity or personal development.

✷ ARCANA 4 ✷

Early family dynamics may have modelled an imbalance of power and responsibility, such as one dominant caregiver and another who was passive or emotionally distant. This can lead to over-self-reliance, difficulty delegating or receiving support, uncertainty around healthy authority or confusion between control and true strength. Growth comes through healing these early imprints with compassion and rebuilding trust in partnership. True maturity requires inner work: learning to guide others calmly, without force or disrespect to heal generational wounds.

✷ ARCANA 5 ✷

You grew up in a rigid household focused on discipline, rules and academic pressure. Control, criticism and constant instruction were common, and emotional distance or family separation may have followed. This pattern may be repeated in your own relationships through dominance, excessive control or rigid expectations. Healing begins with accepting your parents without resentment. Build unity instead of conflict, respect your roots and shape traditions of your own. Lead your family with strength and care, guiding others through example and inspiration rather than pressure or lectures.

✷ ARCANA 6 ✷

As a child, you may have felt unloved or compared your family to others, believing your parents cared for you in the wrong way. This often turns into pride, perfectionism and a need to prove your worth, while still feeling unseen. You may become emotionally dependent on people who reassure you. Healing starts with self-acceptance: valuing yourself without approval. Strengthen your confidence from within, reconnect with your loved ones and make peace with your parents. Build balanced relationships based on reality, not ideals, release perfectionism and learn to notice and appreciate the good in others.

✷ ARCANA 7 ✷

As a child, your boundaries were often ignored, and your parents pushed their own anger and ambitions onto you through harsh pressure. This may have shaped a defensive, impatient mindset: always alert, rushing results and expecting betrayal. Growth comes from redefining strength. Become a leader who guides and supports rather than controls. Motivate others through trust and vision, not fear or criticism, and learn to honour both your own limits and the boundaries of others.

✷ ARCANA 8 ✷

You feel wronged by your parents, and proving yourself may have turned into constant conflict, perhaps even legal battles. At the same time, you may avoid your own duties by not keeping promises or taking responsibility. The way forwards is to drop blame and understand how actions lead to consequences. Let go of old beliefs that no longer work. Speak clearly and fairly, seek understanding and choose discussion and agreement over control or judgement.

✷ ARCANA 9 ✷

Your parents were either emotionally distant or overly controlling, so you wanted to escape early and create a different life. Yet you may be repeating the same patterns without realizing it. To change this, learn to enjoy life's simple pleasures and value material stability without guilt. Trust children's openness, allow closeness and make room for love and friendship. Open your heart and express your feelings honestly.

✷ ARCANA 10 ✷

You grew up under constant supervision, often being seen as incapable and rarely trusted, which may have slowly disconnected you from your own needs. Now you may follow imposed rules, ignore inner signals and believe success only comes through pressure and overwork. Yet in reality, ease suits you better than force. Trust that what genuinely interests you can become stable, rewarding work without burnout. Let go of rigid control, rely more on intuition and choose calm over struggle. When you act with less tension and more trust, life becomes smoother, results come faster and your balanced state positively influences everyone around you.

✷ ARCANA 11 ✷

You were raised under constant pressure to perform, stay busy and outdo others, often through harsh demands. This may have made you driven and demanding, both of yourself and those around you, unable to truly rest. You may push, compete and overwork until exhaustion sets in, leaving projects unfinished. Real progress will come from balance: listening to your body, responding to your basic needs, planning your time and setting clear priorities. Share responsibility, trust others and stop proving your worth through control. Recharge through rest and nature, value abilities over limits and measure yourself by your own capacity, not by comparison.

✷ ARCANA 12 ✷

You grew up learning that love had to be earned, which may have left you feeling unseen and seeking approval through helping others. You may give a lot, expect understanding in return, and feel hurt or resentful when it doesn't come. Saying 'no' feels hard, so you sacrifice yourself and quietly build anger towards both your parents and the people you support. Change begins with valuing yourself. Help only when it feels right and doesn't cost you your peace. Give without expecting anything in return, set clear limits and stop rescuing those who cross boundaries. Choose care over guilt, protect your energy and make space for what genuinely inspires you.

✷ ARCANA 13 ✷

You were raised in a rigid, tradition-bound home, so change may feel threatening rather than hopeful, leaving you holding on to familiar views, avoiding risk and keeping your emotional distance to protect yourself from loss. Growth begins by accepting life as a cycle. Let go of what has passed, allow the new to enter and step forwards without fear. Welcome unfamiliar experiences, even when they feel uncomfortable, because progress often hides inside difficulty. Use your words to encourage and uplift, turning challenge into momentum.

✷ ARCANA 14 ✷

Growing up around addiction is likely to have left you carrying quiet anger and self-doubt, with the sense that your potential has never been fully allowed to unfold. You may take things personally, question your own worth and hold yourself back from joy and self-expression. Healing will come from self-compassion: caring for your inner child, allowing your sensitivity to be expressed and choosing peace over excess. Build warmer family ties, have patience and avoid replacing pain with unhealthy habits. Develop your creative gifts, look beneath the surface of life and trust in the deeper meaning. You can develop strength through self-knowledge, faith, fairness and kindness, treating others with the same care that you seek for yourself.

✷ ARCANA 15 ✷

You are likely to have grown up in a family marked by excess and poor boundaries, and people around you now may be struggling with alcohol, gambling, infidelity or similar addictions. This environment may have shaped a harsh, dominant style: you may push, show aggression, take pride in your achievements and resent others' success, often focusing on their flaws. To truly change your life, face your darker traits honestly and limit any destructive cravings. Transform pride into respect, greed into generosity, aggression into self-control and jealousy into healthy self-confidence. Stop using others' weaknesses for your own advantage; instead, notice their strengths, cooperate with them and learn to genuinely celebrate their successes.

✷ ARCANA 16 ✷

You are meant to guide others, which is why your parents' passivity and pessimism once frustrated you. In rebellion, you may have pushed your limits through your body or excess, searching for strength and meaning. Now, growth may be slowed by self-pity and attachment to material things, but what you cling to most will eventually be taken from you to teach you detachment, and reacting to hardship with anger will only damage close bonds. This path is meant to strengthen your spirit, not break it. Value what you create without holding it tightly, master your emotions and turn aggression into purposeful action.

✷ ARCANA 17 ✷

Your abilities were questioned early on: high demands, little support and constant criticism from your parents may have taught you to downplay your talent. That self-doubt may have followed you into adulthood and kept you from standing out. The way forwards is to be honest with yourself. Develop what you're naturally good at, work consistently and stop waiting for approval or luck. Stay grounded with others, without ego or self-denial, and use your talent as a contribution, not a shield. Choose passion over expectations, let skills grow into meaningful work and fully commit to what excites you. Confidence, recognition and success will follow focused dedication.

⁕ ARCANA 18 ⁕

You were raised under constant parental anxiety, which may have taught you to expect danger and doubt yourself. Now, that worry may have become your own habit and you may fear loss and loneliness. But what you focus on tends to show up fast, both good and bad. This isn't magic, but cause and effect. To move forwards, take responsibility for your thinking, stop living in fear of the past or the future and choose clarity over worry. Work with your inner beliefs, heal anxiety at the root and build a steady mindset so you can live without constant tension or suspicion of the world.

⁕ ARCANA 19 ⁕

As a child, you were overprotected and had mixed feelings about your parents' success. This may still keep you emotionally tied to them and limit your independence. Growth will come through engaging in meaningful activities, ideally those that help others or involve children. Release guilt and self-blame, manage your energy wisely and avoid overinvesting in one area. Let others make their own choices. Real love offers trust, space and respect, not pressure or guidance imposed from above.

⁕ ARCANA 20 ⁕

You grew up in constant conflict with your parents, carrying resentment and a strong urge to escape, which could have led to distance, silence or broken family ties. As this tension may later result in painful dependence instead of freedom, your way forwards is reconciliation, not control. Let go of blame, accept different viewpoints and choose peace. Become the one who unites rather than divides. Acknowledge all family members as part of your story. Healing begins with forgiveness, starting with your parents, and grows through self-awareness, spiritual development and learning to love unconditionally.

⁕ ARCANA 21 ⁕

Having endured restrictive or manipulative parenting, you may find your progress being slowed by financial strain or the rigid beliefs, fear and control you learned from your parents. To move ahead, you need trust, openness and a wider view of life. Step beyond routine, welcome change, explore new places and ideas, and keep learning. Meet differences with respect instead of resistance, take in what's useful and drop what no longer fits. Curiosity, acceptance and connection will foster a full, open life grounded in understanding rather than fear.

⁕ ARCANA 22 ⁕

You were raised under strict control, with little respect for personal space, which may have left you unprepared for responsibility and consistency as an adult. Now, growth will come from respecting others' boundaries while giving yourself more freedom. Loosen rigid rules, stop overthinking and allow creativity, movement, travel and new connections into your life. Take life lightly, face challenges with optimism and humour, and drop inner limits to prevent your own lessons from repeating.

YOUR EXPERIENCE WITH YOUR CHILDREN

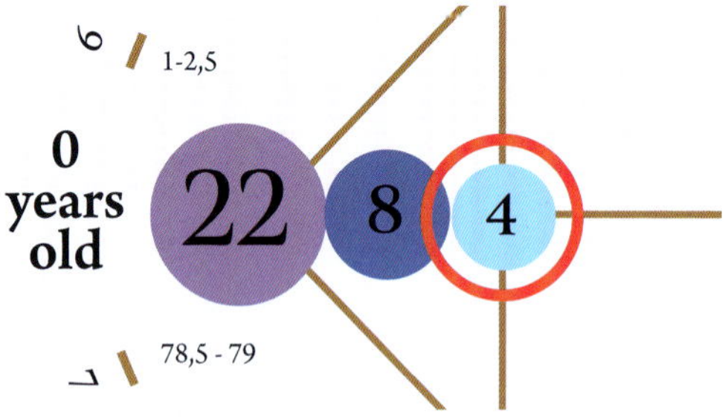

Your Experience With Your Children

✷ ARCANA 2 ✷

Your child will quickly feel when adults aren't sincere. When words clash with actions, it will confuse them. To feel safe, they may adapt, try to please and hide their real emotions. In time, they may get used to doing what is convenient for others and struggle to understand what they truly want. When love flows from fullness, not exhaustion, however, and trust replaces mixed signals, they will begin to speak openly, admit when something is wrong and accept support instead of pretending everything is fine. So, they will learn to express their feelings freely and grow into a calm, confident and balanced adult.

✷ ARCANA 3 ✷

Your child will form their sense of self by observing the emotional atmosphere created by the adults around them. If they see softness, joy, self-respect and ease, rather than control and self-sacrifice, they will absorb this as normal and develop a secure and balanced identity. It is important your child feels trusted and needed and is allowed to contribute in the home. This will help them develop confidence and an understanding that their role matters. Seeing adults treat themselves and each other with care and dignity teaches cooperation instead of power struggles. In turn, your child will become a bridge within the home, awakening tenderness, shared responsibility, courage and unconditional love.

✷ ARCANA 4 ✷

If your child grows up seeing one parent hold all the authority and emotional weight, with little softness or trust in partnership, they will develop distorted expectations: either withdrawing from responsibility or waiting for life to be directed by others. If, on the other hand, there is warmth, trust and emotional openness, they will understand the importance of mutual respect and self-direction. Your child will notice when strength turns rigid and care turns into control, and, alternatively, when gentleness, trust, and cooperation are present. Through their development, a lesson returns to you: balance between structure and tenderness, trust in collaboration and the healthy sharing of responsibility.

✷ ARCANA 5 ✷

If your child grows up surrounded by strict rules, high demands and constant care, they may feel protected yet restrained, which will slow their independence. When adults insist on being right and struggle to bend, children may fear control becoming the norm. Balance will change everything. When respect, dialogue and flexibility replace pressure, your child will learn trust and cooperation. Given space instead of overprotection, they will develop confidence, find their own voice, learn to choose for themselves and have the ability to build relationships without dominance.

✷ ARCANA 6 ✷

If warmth and attention are scarce, your child may feel unseen or inadequate, unable to meet the conditions required to experience love, and their confidence will weaken. Gentle touch, presence and openness, however, will help them feel loved for who they are. When acceptance replaces pressure, they will learn self-worth, trust and balance. They will stop chasing perfection, see beauty in flaws and build relationships without idealizing or rushing. Through this, they will grow grounded, realistic and emotionally secure.

✷ ARCANA 7 ✷

Your child may feel pressured if you push your own dreams onto them, ignoring their own desires and opinions. This can make them defensive, cautious or combative towards the world. When you respect their personal space, however, encourage initiatives and celebrate achievements, they will develop confidence and resilience. Mistakes will become lessons, not punishments. They will learn to grow at their own pace, accept imperfections and navigate challenges with patience and balance.

✷ ARCANA 8 ✷

Your child will feel hurt when promises are broken or commitments are ignored as if fairness doesn't exist. When honesty and consistency are missing, they may struggle with trust and feel compelled to prove themselves. When you as a parent honour their word, take responsibility and respect their perspective, however, they will learn reliability, confidence and self-assurance. They will come to understand cause and effect, value truth and see that fairness comes from actions, not arguments. Through this, they will grow honest, discerning and grounded.

✷ ARCANA 9 ✷

Your child may feel off-balance when at home, sometimes overlooked, sometimes overwhelmed. Too little attention feels like neglect, too much closeness blurs their space. They may dream of leaving early just to breathe. They will become steadier when closeness and distance co-exist. Private space will restore calm, and quiet interest feel safer than control. Trust in life, warmth without pressure, and respect for solitude will help them feel secure. With clear boundaries, they will grow confident and be able to connect with others without losing themselves.

✷ ARCANA 10 ✷

Your child may be labelled as unmotivated, yet they are moving to their own inner rhythm. They will open when choices are truly theirs. Exploration takes time: trying, stopping and changing direction matters more than speed. Pressure will only breed resentment and doubt. And yet your child will notice signs, patterns and quiet knowing. When they are respected, they will grow in confidence; when mocked, they will close off. When ease replaces strain, their direction will become clear. They will thrive in a calm environment, and purpose and creativity will follow naturally.

✷ ARCANA 11 ✷

Your child may grow up under relentless pressure, always being pushed to stay ahead. If so, success will become a race, not a choice, and rest will feel undeserved. They will learn to live in tension. Stress will settle in. Later, they may expect the same effort from others. When ambition softens, however, potential unfolds. Gentleness restores energy. Then emotional control teaches trust, and respect replaces fear. When room is allowed for rest, life feels fuller. When strengths are valued over comparison, your child will grow confident, steady and whole.

✷ ARCANA 12 ✷

Your child may feel loved only when expectations are met. Care may come with conditions, and affection feel tied to performance. The child learns to please just to survive emotionally, burying their own needs. They begin to soften when love is steady and free. Space to choose restores trust. Boundaries allow for self-care. The child may have a natural desire to help and create, and when supported without strings, their creativity will unfold.

✷ ARCANA 13 ✷

Your child may grow up cautious at first, shaped by fear of change and firm traditions. They can seem distant, not from lack of love, but from fear of loss. When change is avoided and truth is softened, their world narrows and anxiety grows. If openness enters the home and endings are spoken honestly, however, they begin to feel safer. Letting go becomes possible. New experiences stop feeling dangerous. In this space, they learn to live in the present, welcome change and move forwards with trust rather than fear.

✷ ARCANA 14 ✷

Your child may notice tension, shaped by your struggles around them. They can feel the weight of unsteady habits and unspoken frustrations. When love and attention are inconsistent, they may carry quiet resentment and doubt their own potential. If you release harmful patterns and bring harmony, patience and support into the home, however, they will begin to feel safer. Calm guidance and belief in their talents will help them grow confident. Gentle boundaries and freedom around choices will allow them to learn balance naturally.

✷ ARCANA 15 ✷

Your child may be shaped by harsh words and volatile moods at home. They will be able to sense aggression and unrest even before they understand it. If control and anger dominate, they may shrink or mimic these patterns. If you learn to manage emotions, let go of addictions and treat others with fairness and compassion, however, they will begin to feel safe. Seeing patience, generosity and respect in action, they will learn to trust relationships.

✷ ARCANA 16 ✷

Your child may feel restless at first, noticing when you resist growth or new experiences. They can push boundaries and explore extremes to find their own path. If guidance is rigid or anger surfaces, they may rebel or withdraw. If you stay curious, calm and open, however, they will begin to feel heard and supported. As they watch patience, love and self-development in action, they learn that challenges are part of life. In this space, they develop resilience and creativity, and learn that every problem can lead to growth, renewal and deeper strength.

✷ ARCANA 17 ✷

Your child may show sparks of talent at first, but without attention and encouragement, those sparks can dim. They can grow frustrated when their interests are ignored or when you compare them to others. They may struggle to express themselves fully or hold back for fear of judgement. When support, belief and respect arrive, however, they will begin to explore their abilities with confidence. Then, they will practise, persevere and develop their gifts, learning that success comes from focus and joy, not comparison. They will dedicate themselves fully to what truly matters, finding fulfilment in the process itself.

✷ ARCANA 18 ✷

Your child may feel smothered at first, surrounded by care that feels too heavy or protective. They can grow anxious, worried about losing loved ones and unsure of their own strength. Yet when love is steady but not controlling, and when you show faith in them, they will begin to trust themselves. The atmosphere around them matters – comfort, order and calm will help their emotions stay balanced. Their thoughts will be quick to shape reality, so guidance and gentle questioning will help them learn discernment. With support, they will begin to rely on their intuition, feel confident in their insights and develop a strong sense of self.

✷ ARCANA 19 ✷

Your child may feel overwhelmed at first, caught in a wave of constant attention and overprotection. They can become dependent, unsure of their own choices and anxious about approval. When given space and trust, however, they will begin to explore independence, make decisions and take responsibility for their actions. Active hobbies, sports, social connections and meaningful projects will help them channel energy productively. With steady support, they will learn to manage emotions and balance their personal drive with care for others.

✷ ARCANA 20 ✷

Your child may sense conflicts and unspoken resentments among family members. They can feel caught in the middle, unsure where to belong and anxious about discord. But when you show unconditional love, seek understanding and model empathy, they will begin to feel safe and connected. Knowing their family history, including any difficult or 'problematic' relatives, will help them understand their roots and themselves. As harmony grows, they will experience the warmth of belonging, learn to navigate relationships with patience and care, and feel the security of being part of a family that values connection, forgiveness and closeness.

✷ ARCANA 21 ✷

Your child may feel restricted at first, sensing rules, limits and tension around money or authority. They can feel frustrated, boxed in or hesitant to explore their own ideas. When you trust them, encourage dreaming and support their endeavours, however, they will begin to feel free and capable. Shared imagination, bold goals and openness to new experiences will help them expand their thinking and embrace possibilities. When curiosity, respect and exploration are welcomed, they will grow confident and adventurous and be connected to the wider world, feeling that nothing is out of reach.

✷ ARCANA 22 ✷

Your child may feel restricted at first, sensing strict rules and boundaries that leave little room for freedom. They can react with rebellion, testing limits and seeking space to explore. If you respect their independence, offer support and engage in shared creative activities, they will begin to trust. Humour, curiosity and enjoyment of life will help them navigate challenges lightly, while seeing responsibility in action will teach balance. Active family experiences, travel and new discoveries will expand their worldview and spark creativity. Slowly, they will learn to move confidently, embrace freedom and approach life with openness and resilience.

CHAPTER 5

YOUR GIFTS

YOUR CONNECTION TO THE UNIVERSE

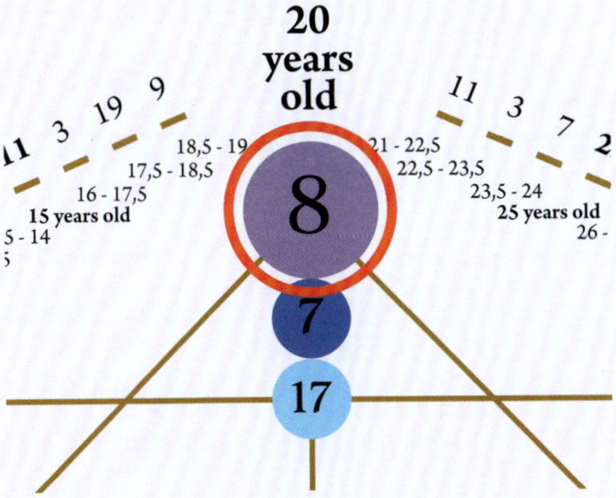

Your Connection to the Universe

The second basic energy in the Matrix is your birth month, often referred to as the 'channel of intuition', which represents the spiritual aspect of your personality and governs your connection with the Divine, whether you think of that as God, the universe or the Absolute, according to your own understanding. When this energy is lived positively, it allows you to receive guidance from the universe. This connection leads to spiritual wholeness, greater success and a sense of ease in life, as you learn to trust the world around you. However, when this energy is at a low level, there is a lack of belief in higher powers or trust in the universe. You may feel disconnected from anything higher, and everything in life may seem to require struggle and effort. In such cases, it is important to understand that life's challenges are not meant to punish you, but to guide you back to your soul's natural path.

Your divine connection is part of your soul's gifts, and we will look at these in more detail now.

YOUR TALENTS

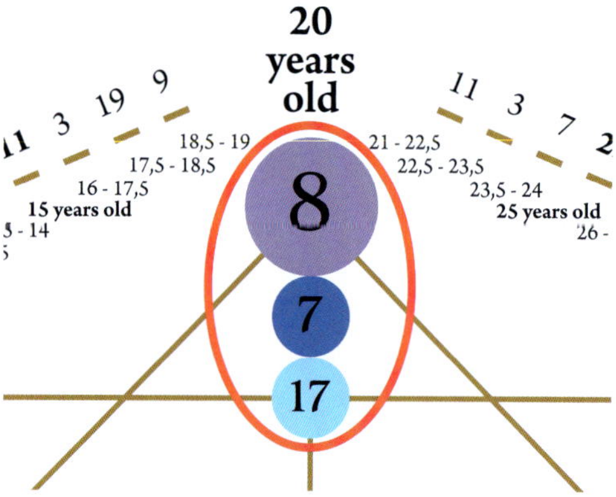

Your Talents

Every person has innate talents, their soul's natural gifts. These may stem from past lives or be inherited through the family lineage. Your task is to uncover and develop your own abilities, as they play a crucial role in creative pursuits, self-realization, work, communication and achievements. It is essential to recognize your talents and make a conscious effort to regularly express them in daily life.

✷ ARCANA 1 ✷

You possess unique gifts and instincts suited for leadership and spiritual guidance. Your quick-thinking mind translates thoughts into actions, helping you manifest ideas and transmit knowledge, choosing your associates carefully. You excel in communication, initiate projects and create connections seamlessly. At your core lies a deep spiritual belief rooted in nature, alongside intuitive healing abilities linked to the Earth and its energies. As a natural teacher and guide, you may sometimes feel restrained by your ego or past obligations, yet these are integral to your identity.

✷ ARCANA 2 ✷

You possess unique gifts as a natural leader and guide, particularly in spiritual matters. Your discerning nature allows you to resonate with true authenticity and your mental acuity drives your thoughts into action. You learn rapidly and communicate effectively, fostering connections and ease in projects. Your intuition is strong, often allowing you to perceive truths others overlook. With a calming presence and diplomatic skills, you subtly guide outcomes while demonstrating empathy. Your prophetic dreams and adeptness in esoteric practices highlight your role as a spiritual guide. You possess a deep spiritual connection to nature and your ancestry, and can heal and activate inherited gifts. However, obstacles like ego or emotional blocks can weaken your power if not addressed.

✷ ARCANA 3 ✷

You possess a fertile creative energy that fosters growth in people, projects and environments through your nurturing and inspiring presence. Your refined aesthetic sense and intuitive support, particularly within the family and partnerships, enhance the abundance around you. This abundance flows best when you're engaged in work you enjoy, particularly in artistic or healing endeavours. Grounded in Earth energy and maternal care, your gifts derive from ancestral wisdom, enabling you to anchor peace and healing in your community. When balanced, you attract beauty and prosperity effortlessly; however, the avoidance of responsibility or disconnection from your creative essence can lead to strain and depletion. Your journey calls for the full awakening of your creative authority and nurturing power.

✷ ARCANA 4 ✷

You possess strong leadership energy, with an innate capacity to establish companies and systems. Management and organization come naturally to you, allowing you to influence environments and adapt structures effectively. With the ability to learn quickly, you blend strategic thinking with negotiation skills to protect your interests and those of your team. You plan ahead, make decisive moves and take responsibility, driven by a sharp business sense for profit and long-term growth. Connected to Earth and ancestral traditions, you embody wisdom and have a deep responsibility for transmitting sacred knowledge. Your leadership in spiritual spaces brings clarity to teachings and communities. However, you must balance your strength with wisdom to avoid rigidity and burnout as you fully embrace your role as a builder and keeper of wisdom.

✷ ARCANA 5 ✷

You possess a remarkable talent for eloquence and persuasion, excelling in teaching and forming communities of like-minded individuals. Your approach to knowledge is experiential, filtering ideas through direct experience and practical methods. You organize and simplify complex information, making it accessible. Your skills in research, analysis and synthesis lead to clear, usable insights. As a natural teacher and mentor, you attract students while continually learning. Public speaking is a strength, empowering others to express themselves too. You embody the spirit of a teacher and draw wisdom from diverse spiritual traditions, using your intuitive abilities for emotional and physical healing. However, growth can be hindered by clinging to old beliefs or resisting new ideas.

✷ ARCANA 6 ✷

You possess a natural affinity for beauty and harmony, which allows you to transform elegance into value and income. Your presence fosters balance and strong, harmonious relationships. With diplomatic skills and emotional intelligence, you ease tensions and help others feel appreciated. You inspire people to showcase their best qualities, with communication characterized by charm and warmth. Guided by love and empathy, you uplift others, assisting them in making clear decisions and enjoying life. This heart-centred approach makes you a focal point in communities, drawing like-minded individuals together for a shared purpose. However, when blocked, tendencies towards idealization and imitation can hinder the expression of your gifts.

✷ ARCANA 7 ✷

You possess a unique ability to transform a vision into reality through determination and persistence, consistently working towards significant goals while believing in success. Your natural leadership skills enable you to inspire and guide others. You approach challenges strategically, prioritizing results and effectively managing processes. With adaptability and a focus on innovation, you solve problems using rational thought. You effectively channel inner aggression into disciplined effort, blending power with spiritual principles in a way that makes you a mentor and guide to others. However, obstacles such as impatience, isolation or stagnation may hinder your progress.

✷ ARCANA 8 ✷

You possess objective judgement and impartiality, with a keen understanding of cause and effect and karmic law. This allows you to strategize effectively, maintain composure under pressure and coordinate complex tasks with clarity and integrity. You are guided by a strong sense of justice and are drawn to reflection and spiritual discipline. When aligned with universal principles, you can inspire and elevate others through your wisdom; however, blockages such as deception or rigid judgement can hinder your effectiveness.

✷ ARCANA 9 ✷

You embody self-sufficiency, integrity and wisdom, thriving in your inner world. Your sharp mind quickly grasps profound truths, allowing you to master various pursuits through insight and disciplined thought. You perceive life holistically, learning from past errors to heal others and environments. Your gift of communication shines in intimate settings, where your insights resonate deeply. Your essence is rooted in devotion, spiritual discipline and an understanding of higher laws. Research and reflection come naturally to you, as you draw from your experiences and ancient wisdom. Healing is integral to your identity; you work intuitively with nature and energies. Your connection to the spiritual realm gives you strength, while you approach relationships with care and consistency. However, obstacles like isolation or self-doubt can affect your abilities.

✷ ARCANA 10 ✷

You possess strong intuition and a good sense of timing, which allow you to navigate life effectively. By setting intentions, you create favourable circumstances and help others find direction and opportunities. You attract resources effortlessly and generate original projects without forcing results. Trusting your instincts and adapting to life's cycles, you embrace both challenges and growth. Your core strength lies in your spiritual connection and ability to communicate inspiringly. Your path is one of spiritual purpose and self-understanding, facilitating healing, guidance and leadership naturally. However, being overly focused on money or rigid structures may hinder your flow.

✷ ARCANA 11 ✷

You possess a powerful and motivating energy that inspires both yourself and others to achieve goals. You combine physical strength, emotional depth and spiritual power, all of which enable you to manage multiple demands effectively. Your commitment to your goals utilizes all your resources, leading to high performance and quick recovery. With natural healing abilities, you easily restore balance and vitality, transforming any starting point into a meaningful outcome. As a leader, your consistency and clarity foster belief in others, empowering them to realize their potential. You communicate sincerely and uphold your values, using your influence to support and heal. Your soul's connection to nature and ancestral wisdom enhances your intuition and healing capabilities through Earth-based practices. Engaging in prayer and ritual opens pathways to insights that guide both you and others, though neglecting bodily signals and overexertion can sap your strength.

✷ ARCANA 12 ✷

You possess a unique creative perspective that enables you to uncover original meanings in various aspects of life. You effortlessly blend ideas with the ability to organize experiences and emotions into practical outcomes. Your deep emotional understanding fosters empathy and wisdom, allowing you to offer unconventional yet accurate guidance. Driven by compassion, you are committed to serving people, animals and the world. Your creative expressions, particularly through your voice, serve as channels for influence and healing. Your connection to your family and ancestry guides your nurturing role, with an emphasis on providing balance and stability. However, challenges may arise when you find yourself in disempowered or co-dependent dynamics, which can obscure your light.

CHAPTER 6

YOUR KARMA

YOUR KARMIC TAIL

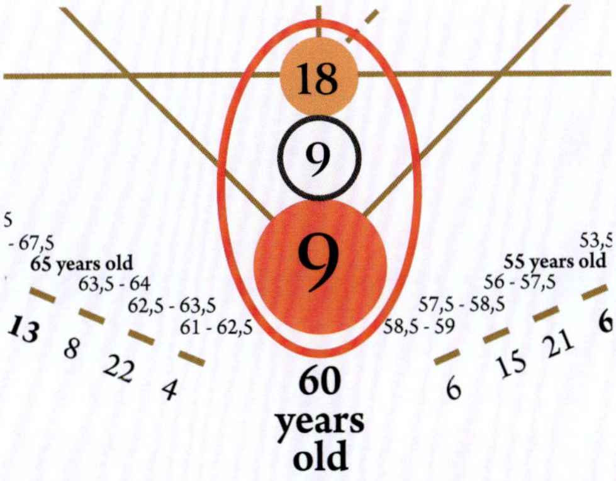

Your Karmic Tail

Your Karmic Tail is found at the bottom of the Matrix and consists of three numbers that form a unified 'program'. This reveals who your soul was in a past incarnation, how it interacted with others and how these past experiences may be affecting your present life. By understanding your Karmic Tail, you can recognize recurring patterns, challenges and lessons that need to be addressed. It provides guidance on what actions can be taken to resolve unfinished karma, break negative cycles and move towards greater personal and spiritual growth.

The numerical combinations may seem arbitrary, but only these combinations are possible in chart readings.

✷ 18-6-6 ✷

Your Karmic Tail describes a past life where you experienced unrequited love, leading to a reliance on love magic which deprived the other of free will. This resulted in a profound loss of self-worth. In your current life, you may find yourself in a family lacking love, which drives a relentless quest for affection. As an adult, you may rush from partner to partner, seeking validation and entering unsuitable relationships which only reinforce feelings of inadequacy. Unreciprocated love re-enacts past experiences, creating a dependency on others for self-worth and resulting in an endless cycle of dissatisfaction.

The lesson is to cultivate self-love, recognize your personal worth and seek happiness independently, thus avoiding the manipulation of others. Fostering stable, healthy relationships and focusing on internal joy are essential for breaking this cycle.

✵ 18-9-9 or 9-9-18 ✵

In a past life, you experienced deep knowledge and solitude yet chose not to share your insights due to doubts about their value and fears of causing harm. This led to a persistent belief in your unworthiness and a fear of transmitting what you know. In this life, you still possess such knowledge but may struggle with its application and the balance between solitude, which allows for deep work, and the need for close relationships. You often immerse yourself in study to avoid engaging with the world, doubting the utility of your experiences. Loneliness is familiar, yet you fear it, seeking validation from others instead of self-belief.

The karmic lesson is to believe in your knowledge and share it despite uncertainties. This will foster both personal growth and fulfilling relationships. Accept your unique knowledge and learn to trust your intuition, allowing for interaction rather than retreating into isolation.

✵ 9-18-9 ✵

In a past life, you may have acquired deep knowledge while living in seclusion, fearing that your abilities could harm others, which led to loneliness and self-doubt. Currently, you still possess knowledge but may hesitate to use it, feeling the need for solitude to study while also longing for close relationships. You often immerse yourself in learning to avoid engaging with the world, doubting the value of your experiences.

The challenge is to believe in yourself without seeking validation from others. It's crucial for you to accept and share your unique knowledge, trust your intuition and embrace opportunities that arise from it. Learning to connect with others while managing your fears of loneliness is essential for personal growth and fulfilment.

✵ 15-20-5 ✵

In a past life, you separated from your powerful family due to conflicting beliefs, leading to guilt and a desire for atonement. In this life, born into a fractured family, you embody the 'Rebel', facing two potential scenarios. In the first, you maintain past patterns, holding strong personal beliefs, distancing yourself from your family and rejecting their values, while facing increasing difficulties. In the second, you focus on family unity, sacrificing your personal beliefs to mend ties and uphold traditions, yet feeling a sense of loss.

The karmic lesson is to find a balance between your personal beliefs and family interests, restore communication, accept support and contribute to the family lineage without losing yourself. Recognizing the need to reconnect with excluded family members and foster unity is essential for your growth and fulfilment.

✵ 15-5-8 ✵

In a previous life, you led an immoral lifestyle, which could manifest in your current life through repeated cycles of betrayal and temptation, or attracting partners with past addictions. If you indulge in infidelity or chase new relationships, you may experience doubts, particularly in youth or around the age of 40, requiring a choice between stability and passion. Alternatively, if you strive for honesty, you might still encounter individuals with the same addictions you once had, leading to emotional betrayal.

The key lesson is to cultivate understanding and forgiveness of those who have hurt you, rather than attempting to change them. Recognizing and releasing rigid expectations can also help prevent attracting betrayal. Appreciate the love you already have in your life. Eventually, self-forgiveness will enable true empathy and closure of this cycle of karma.

✷ 18-3-12 ✷

In previous lifetimes, you may have felt imprisoned by physical limitations, leading to a karmic influence characterized by the roles of victim and rescuer. As a victim, you may seek sympathy and attention, sometimes even manifesting illness to create a familiar dynamic. As a rescuer, you become overly involved in the health crises of others, while failing to recognize when genuine support is needed rather than constant care. These patterns may result in self-harm or emotional distress.

You must learn to consciously work through these karmic roles by providing the appropriate psychological and moral support without losing your own identity. Maintaining a balance between caring for others and self-care is crucial, along with acknowledging that illnesses reflect a person's inner state and are tied to psychosomatic principles. Recognizing that true assistance involves guiding others to acceptance rather than fighting against their condition is essential for spiritual growth.

✷ 15-8-11 ✷

In past lives, you were aggressive and domineering, causing suffering to others, and now you carry the karmic burden of that pain. In this life, you may have a physically weaker body but retain inner strength and ambition. You might also experience feelings of powerlessness and aggression from others. Parenting may pose challenges if your child doesn't meet your expectations, potentially igniting aggression towards them. If these lessons are unheeded, physical consequences may occur, indicating a need for change.

Your main lesson is to control your inner aggression to prevent it from manifesting physically. Learning to defend yourself, preferably through martial arts, will help you recognize that acting out of aggression leads to negative outcomes. The goal is to embrace different perspectives, using physical activity as a means of balancing your energies.

✷ 9-15-6 ✷

In previous incarnations, you experienced a rich inner world filled with vivid fantasies, yet faced rejection and criticism from society, leading to feelings of shame and internal suppression. This resulted in destructive behaviours, including substance abuse and unhealthy relationships. Currently, you may find yourself with a similar inner depth, which again feels disconnected from reality. If suppressed, it may drive you towards destructive outlets.

The task of this life is to channel this energy into creativity and love, learning to express your uniqueness while finding a balance between reality and imagination. The journey involves overcoming shame and accepting that being truthful to yourself is paramount, despite societal expectations. Additionally, forgiving those who inflict pain through their own struggles can aid in fulfilling your karmic purpose and help you realize your potential.

✷ 6-17-11 ✷

In the past, you had immense talent and potential, but chose a conventional life due to external pressures, suppressing your abilities. Currently, you tend to avoid fully engaging with your skills, opting for safer professions, but, despite distractions and responsibilities, such as providing for your children, you often feel unfulfilled and may consider your ideas worthless. Financial constraints can also impede your self-realization, leading to prioritizing realism over dreams.

The lesson is to recognize and develop your talents, focusing on self-fulfilment rather than others' expectations. It is essential to reflect on your aspirations, claim your path and persist in pursuing your goals, even if success isn't immediate.

✷ 12-19-7 ✷

In a previous life, you were a powerful warrior who inflicted harm and suffering through conquest without fully comprehending the consequences. This led to an internal conflict as you recognized the pain caused and chose to renounce taking sides. In this life, you possess great potential as a leader but are torn between the desire to achieve and the fear of causing harm. This may manifest as aggression or conflict avoidance.

You are encouraged to examine your goals for any destructive potential and to pursue creative, peaceful resolutions instead. Focusing on global objectives and understanding multiple perspectives can help you channel your warrior spirit into constructive efforts. Ultimately, you are called to transform past violence into acts of service, balancing ambition with ethical responsibility.

✷ 9-12-3 ✷

In a past life, you were a woman who suffered from loneliness and unfulfilled love, often tied to loss or abandonment and a deep attachment to your mother. You either focused on saving others or clung to one lost love, neglecting your own happiness and personal fulfilment. In this life, you may struggle with loneliness and depression and have difficulty forming lasting relationships, often choosing partners or situations that keep you overly reliant on a maternal figure or tied to the past.

The lesson is to love yourself, stop depending on a partner or a maternal figure for meaning, embrace independence, pursue your own happiness and open your heart to new relationships while taking responsibility for your life.

✷ 6-5-17 ✷

In your past life, you were born with remarkable gifts that made you prideful and led to a sense of superiority, ultimately resulting in rejection from your family and society. In this

incarnation you may again possess talents that provoke envy and humiliation. Your challenges include doubting your abilities and seeking validation from others, leading to success that is hard-earned and a painful relationship with perceived advantages.

To break this karmic cycle, you must reconnect with your true goals and values, earn your success independently and transform pride into humility. This allows for genuine personal growth, fostering a sense of achievement through patience and effort. Your journey emphasizes mutual respect and equality with others, facilitating the healing of pride for a fulfilled existence.

✷ 21-4-10 ✷

In a past life, you experienced conditions of severe oppression and accepted a secondary role, leading to inner self-doubt and a choice to remain subjugated. This pattern is re-emerging in your present life, where you are often devalued and feel that decisions are made by others, which causes you to feel insecure and rely on external validation. You find it challenging to assert yourself or take independent actions, so often seek a protector, but feel confined when pressured.

The lesson is to believe in yourself, take independent steps and remove internal limitations. Realize that success comes with freedom and it is normal to achieve without excessive struggle. Your goals are valid and mistakes are a part of growth. Your life is in your own hands and you may pursue whatever it is that your soul desires.

✷ 12-16-4 ✷

In a past life, you were a powerful conqueror, exerting control over resources and people, driven by a hunger for power. This led to destruction and an inner sense of insignificance, prompting a decision to seek true dignity. In your current life, a gentle or fragile exterior may hide an inner strength capable of commanding. You may feel compelled to control others but often face setbacks as life resists your attempts at domination. Your desire for control can also lead to destructive behaviour when you are faced with vulnerability.

The lesson is to release control, embrace humility and trust life's unfolding, recognizing others' independence while balancing personal and collective interests, and leading through trust and love rather than domination.

✷ 3-22-19 ✷

In a past life, your soul may have experienced early death or non-birth (through a pressured abortion or miscarriage), resulting in an unresolved yearning for maternal love. This unfulfilled need can manifest in your current life as a tendency to move quickly through experiences, a fear of sudden life endings and an emotional distance from a maternal figure. You may seek maternal affection from others while remaining emotionally immature and struggling to achieve independence.

The central lesson involves forgiving your mother, ceasing to seek love from external sources and learning to cultivate self-love. Healing is achieved by embracing life, allowing yourself a 'second childhood' and, for some women, through the conscious choice of motherhood, eventually restoring self-love, stability and well-being.

✷ 21-10-16 ✷

In your past life, you were a vessel of spiritual knowledge, possibly serving as a leader or priest, but you halted your mission due to the negative impact of your teachings. In this life, you possess wisdom and the ability to convey spiritual insights but are afraid that your knowledge might harm others. This fear may lead to self-doubt and prevent you from realizing your full potential.

Embracing your role as a guide is crucial; neglecting it will result in feelings of stagnation. Your mission involves revealing spiritual knowledge rather than mastering a craft, with careers in psychology, astrology and similar fields aligning with this path. Your karmic lesson is to acknowledge your influence and leadership, which will allow you to travel and learn from diverse experiences. It is important to share your knowledge without feeling responsible for its application by others. Embrace your mission, declare your insights confidently and understand that you are not responsible for how others utilize the information you provide.

✷ 6-8-20 ✷

In a past life, you were the heir of a prestigious family, but, as your soul chose to teach acceptance and unconditional love within the family, you became a 'black sheep' by following your own path. In this life, your family may again expect much from you, and from an early age you may strive to prove your worth. This pursuit can exhaust you, and you learn that you deserve love simply for being yourself, not for meeting the expectations of others.

Your karmic lesson is to honour your own desires and self-worth while healing family relationships. By following your true passions, you can achieve success, elevate the family's legacy and influence future generations. Focus on excelling in one area, avoid perfectionism and encourage independence in others, especially those with challenges, to continue the family's healing. In some cases, perceived weakness or limitations may bring your family together, teaching them unconditional love.

✷ 3-7-22 ✷

In a previous life, you experienced confinement, which shaped your routines and created a deep yearning for liberation. In this life, you may confront various limitations, beginning in childhood with dietary habits and extending into adulthood with unforeseen obstacles or dependence on medication. You have a calling to inspire hope, potentially through professions that advocate for personal liberty. However, there is a risk of relinquishing responsibility to others, leading to feelings of imprisonment. Your lesson is to understand that true freedom is an internal pursuit that transcends physical and moral constraints. Embracing this notion requires accepting limitations while focusing on spiritual growth, thereby allowing for recovery and the ability to live authentically without excessive reliance on structure or distractions.

✷ 9-3-21 ✷

In a past life, you exerted control over others while having an underlying fear of losing your own status. This often led to mocking or manipulating behaviours as a form of self-protection. In your current life, tendencies to control or manipulate may persist, providing a false sense of superiority or security. However, the potential loss of status, wealth or power illustrates the consequences of such domination.

The lesson is to learn the importance of respecting others' freedoms and boundaries, avoiding dependency and providing help without expectation of repayment. Additionally, forgiving debts, honouring agreements, fostering balanced relationships based on nobility rather than dominance and letting go of the fear of falling in status are crucial. Then, you transform your relationship with power and learn true responsibility.

✷ 21-7-13 ✷

In a past life, you were a military leader involved in the creation of weapons but deeply affected by the death of loved ones. This led to a soul decision to seek restoration and protection for those lost. In this life, you may be drawn to roles that help and save others, such as a doctor or firefighter, focusing on selfless service and compassion without seeking personal gain. Challenges may arise, however, including temptations to engage in harmful work. You may be encouraged to intervene in life-or-death situations but must learn to respect the natural course of life.

Your path involves helping others but understanding your limits and accepting that you cannot save everyone, maintaining a balance between effort and acceptance.

✷ 18-6-15 ✷

In a previous existence, you wielded potent magical powers to influence others covertly for personal gain, often harming individuals without consent. Fearful of mass impact, you ultimately chose to reclaim your power. In your current life, you possess a magical gift and may encounter ongoing temptations to misuse it for control or harm, motivated by desires for power and material wealth. So, while you may project charm and positivity, your underlying motives can include revenge and control.

Your lesson is to learn to not interfere in others' affairs, use your abilities responsibly and respect higher forces. Ethical living through cooperation and mutual benefit is crucial to avoid negative karmic consequences from the misuse of power.

✷ 6-20-14 ✷

In a past life, you acted selflessly for your family or community, but your sacrifices went unrecognized, leading to feelings of futility. In this life, you experience ease and support, attracting success and opportunities seemingly effortlessly, which can evoke envy. However, feelings of guilt may lead you to justify your actions through over-generosity.

Your lesson is to appreciate the gifts life offers, acknowledge the contributions of others and practise moderation. Avoid indiscriminate helping and focus on personal growth, recognizing that you don't owe anyone anything and that true fulfilment comes from gratitude and love.

✷ 21-10-7 ✷

In a previous life, you actively imposed beliefs, sometimes using force, thinking it was for the good while ignoring that goodness cannot be forced. In this life, you may feel a strong urge to persuade others, potentially affecting personal relationships. This propensity to impose your ideals stems from a desire for validation and recognition and often results in actions that do not reflect your true self. You have an impulse to help others without being asked, which can lead to a backlash if such help is unwelcome.

Your karmic lesson is to allow others their independence, to refrain from imposing your views and to accept differing perspectives. Your current task is to embody your values through authentic service and setting an example, rather than aggression or coercion, acknowledging that true recognition comes from living authentically rather than copying others or promoting ideals that are not aligned with your real self.

✷ 3-13-10 ✷

In a past life, you may have rejected life when challenges felt overwhelming, choosing the seemingly easier path of death. In this life, you may face early struggles, which may include difficulties surrounding your birth or a tendency towards reckless behaviour, a lack of regard for your body and situations that test your resilience and survival. You may also experience apathy, depression or fear of challenges, avoid responsibility and question the meaning of life.

Your karmic lesson is to value and embrace life, confront challenges, take responsibility for your actions, seek help when needed and live fully in the present. By learning from hardships and inspiring others, you will come to understand that the meaning of life lies in living it fully and positively. You are encouraged to cultivate gratitude for the lessons life brings and to foster resilience in both yourself and those around you.

✷ 6-14-8 ✷

In a past life, you were a dictator, accustomed to power and control, but faced limitations that led to inner torment and a desire for revenge. In this life, authoritarian dynamics from early family experiences may have influenced your tendency to conceal your true self, leading to a belief that others are seeking to undermine you. Despite your capacity to shape global situations, you prefer a modest life, working behind the scenes.

Your karmic task is to use your power responsibly, exerting a only gentle influence and considering the consequences of your actions. You heal by focusing on regaining self-respect, avoiding pride and despotism, and dedicating yourself to good deeds, while acknowledging that your leadership energy remains impactful.

YOUR ANCESTRAL KARMA

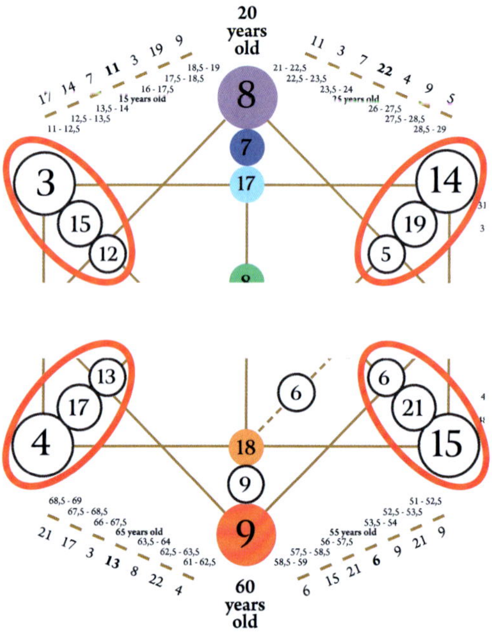

Your Ancestral Karma

These diagonals represent inherited karmic patterns across generations. The left diagonal (top to bottom: 3–15–12) reflects the paternal line's material karma (father, grandfather and great-grandfather) passed down to the kin. The right diagonal (bottom to top: 15–21–6) represents the paternal line's spiritual karma (father, grandfather and great-grandfather) passed down to the kin. Similarly, on the maternal side, the right diagonal (top to bottom: 14–19–5) shows the maternal line's material karma (mother, grandmother and great-grandmother) passed down to the kin. The left diagonal (bottom to top: 4–17–13) represents the maternal line's spiritual karma (mother, grandmother, and great-grandmother) inherited by the kin.

✷ ARCANA 2 ✷

You carry an ancient gift for harmonizing opposites, healing conflicts and sensing deeper truth through intuition and dreams, and you are invited to use it to unite your mother's and father's family lines and restore peace within your family system. When this gift is blocked, you may feel divided, indecisive, lazy or stuck between choices.

Heal this karma by seeking balance, releasing family conflicts and trusting your inner guidance. By doing so, you will gain strength and wisdom from your ancestors, attract a compatible soul partner and have stable, harmonious relationships.

✷ ARCANA 3 ✷

Your ancestral karma is connected to the strong feminine energy in your family line. You carry the gift of nurturing, protecting and creating stability in home, health and material life, along with natural leadership abilities. When this energy is unbalanced, it can show up as control issues, dependence or tension with family.

Heal this karma by respecting the feminine, healing your relationship with a maternal figure, releasing control, allowing children and loved ones to grow freely and staying connected to nature and meaningful work.

✷ ARCANA 4 ✷

Your ancestral karma is connected to your father's line and also to the masculine energy in your family. You carry lessons about authority, responsibility, leadership and building a stable material foundation. When this energy is unbalanced, it can show up as control, aggression, fear of responsibility or conflict with paternal figures.

Heal this karma by allowing others to make their own decisions, accepting leadership and professional growth, leading with fairness and empathy, healing your relationship with a father figure and staying flexible.

✷ ARCANA 5 ✷

Your ancestral karma is about family laws, traditions, responsibility and maintaining order. You carry the role of a keeper of values, knowledge and structure, with a natural ability to teach, guide and hold authority in social or family systems. When this is unbalanced, it can show up as rigidity, pride, moral pressure, control or conflicts around marriage and trust.

Heal this karma by respecting others' opinions, honouring family traditions and the law, releasing pride and spiritual ego, avoiding preaching, staying flexible and open, trusting your family's choices and bringing relatives together.

✷ ARCANA 6 ✷

Your ancestral karma is about love, relationships and family connections. You carry the energy that nurtures children, unites partners and brings warmth and harmony to your family. When this is blocked, it can show up as indecisiveness, emotional lack or unrealistic expectations in relationships.

Heal this karma by loving yourself as you are, doing things that fulfil you, stopping idealizing your partner, making decisions from your heart, accepting your flaws, releasing fear of mistakes and being gentle with yourself and others.

✷ ARCANA 7 ✷

Your ancestral karma is about action, drive and leadership. You carry the energy that motivates movement, achievement and guiding others, but if unhealed, it can appear as aggression, competitiveness or difficulty enjoying success.

Heal this karma by overcoming laziness, setting ambitious but peaceful goals, delegating to and trusting others, taking charge of your life, travelling and gaining perspective, acting on intuition and accepting life's cycles.

✷ ARCANA 8 ✷

Your ancestral karma is about balance, justice and taking responsibility for karmic lessons. You carry the energy to set things right in your family, heal past harms and use your strength wisely. When unhealed, it can show as aggression, blame or a constant struggle with injustice.

Heal this karma by using your strength for good, demonstrating patience and tolerance, leading with inspiration, avoiding imposing yourself on others, balancing work and rest, and spending time in nature and with animals.

✷ ARCANA 9 ✷

Your ancestral karma is about wisdom, spiritual connection and sharing the deep knowledge of your family line. You carry the gift of healing and insight and the ability to unite people through shared values and spiritual understanding. When this is blocked, it can show as isolation, fear of judgement or holding back your knowledge.

Heal this karma by spending time in solitude but staying connected, sharing your wisdom with others, following your curiosity, opening up emotionally, connecting with like-minded people, enjoying nature and committing to self-discovery and growth.

✷ ARCANA 10 ✷

Your ancestral karma is about destiny, life flow and guiding the family's souls through the cycles of rebirth. You carry the energy to trust life, follow your intuition and release control over what cannot be managed. When this energy is blocked, it can show as worry, distrust, over-effort or being swept along others' paths.

Heal this karma by trusting life, listening to your intuition, following your true desires, believing in abundance, travelling and expanding your perspective, acting on inspiration and accepting life's cycles.

✷ ARCANA 11 ✷

Your ancestral karma is about strength, vitality and the support passed down from both your maternal and paternal lines. You carry the energy for creativity, sexual potency, stamina and connection to natural forces, along with the potential to inspire and lead. When unhealed, this can show as aggression, cruelty or the misuse of power.

Heal this karma by using your strength for good, demonstrating patience and tolerance, leading by inspiring others, communicating softly without force, respecting others' pace, balancing work and rest, and connecting with nature and animals.

✷ ARCANA 12 ✷

Your ancestral karma is about service, compassion and supporting others within your family and society. You carry the energy to teach, mentor and offer help with love and integrity. When this is blocked, it can show as learned helplessness, over-identifying with suffering or trying to control others.

Heal this karma by serving others selflessly, stepping into your power, setting healthy boundaries, helping only when needed and offering support with love and clarity.

✷ ARCANA 13 ✷

Your ancestral karma is about seniority, protection and guiding the cycle of life and death. You carry the energy to support family members, assist with major life changes and help release and heal ancestral souls. When this is blocked, it can show as fear of change, attachment or resistance to life's cycles.

Heal this karma by letting go of attachments, embracing change, loving life fully, being tactful and compassionate, renewing yourself regularly and helping ancestors through prayers or rituals.

✷ ARCANA 14 ✷

Your ancestral karma is about creative power, emotional healing and connecting with the spiritual knowledge of your family line. You carry the energy to release trapped souls, overcome addictions and work with angelic guidance. When this is blocked, it can show as emotional struggles, attachment or repeating past patterns of suffering.

Heal this karma by connecting with your soul, letting go of grudges and resentment, detaching from others' negativity, exploring your spiritual growth, expressing your creativity and caring for your health and body.

✷ ARCANA 15 ✷

Your ancestral karma is about spiritual light, leadership, intuition and the power to transform your family's legacy. You carry the gifts of prophecy and clairvoyance and have psychic abilities, but also inherited challenges like pride, aggression, addictions and entanglement in negative energies.

Heal this karma by pursuing spiritual growth, resisting life's temptations, being honest with yourself and others, releasing addictions and limitations, avoiding manipulating others, controlling aggression, communicating with tact and staying away from harmful or illegal actions.

✷ ARCANA 16 ✷

Your ancestral karma is about spiritual awakening, healing and the gift of teaching. You carry the energy to transform your family, share wisdom and grow spiritually. When blocked, this can show as attachment, clinging or repeating destructive cycles.

Heal this karma by developing spiritually, forgiving yourself and your parents, accepting life changes and losses, avoiding attachment and routine, releasing what no longer serves you and connecting with sacred spaces and ancestor energy.

✷ ARCANA 17 ✷

Your ancestral karma is about stardom, talent and creative gifts. You carry the energy to express your abilities, grow professionally and develop a unique potential. When blocked, this can show as pride, arrogance, envy or unfulfilled talent.

Heal this karma by forgiving your parents and ancestors, accepting your childhood experiences, having self-love, discovering and refining your talents, staying humble, avoiding envy and embracing creativity and adventure.

✷ ARCANA 18 ✷

Your ancestral karma is about magic, mysticism and lunar energy. You carry the gifts of imagination, sensitivity, creativity and prophetic vision. When blocked, these can appear as fear, negative thinking, mental turmoil or misused magic.

Heal this karma by managing your thoughts, cultivating positivity, trusting your intuition, avoiding harmful practices, visualizing success, being honest with yourself and others, and slowly releasing ancestral burdens.

✷ ARCANA 19 ✷

Your ancestral karma is about social service, leadership and political or creative influence. You carry the gifts of eloquence, creativity and intuition, and the ability to serve society. When blocked, these can show as inner aggression, dissatisfaction, pride, pessimism or discord in relationships.

Heal this karma by transforming negative energy into inspiration, releasing guilt, connecting with your inner child, being generous and positive, reconciling with your siblings and family, avoiding obsession and committing to spiritual growth and service.

✷ ARCANA 20 ✷

Your ancestral karma is about spiritual clairvoyance, connecting with your remote ancestors and receiving divine knowledge. You carry prophetic gifts, intuition and the ability to sense subtle spiritual worlds. When blocked, these can appear as family conflict, distrust, judgement or disharmony.

Heal this karma by accepting yourself and your family unconditionally, cultivating respect, helping and receiving help from your relatives, honouring your ancestors as well as your homeland, developing your extrasensory abilities and caring for your family graves and legacies.

✷ ARCANA 21 ✷

Your ancestral karma is about global service, peacekeeping and connecting with the world and universe. You carry the energy to unite people, serve society and bring belligerent or intolerant family energies into harmony. When blocked, this can show as rigidity, intolerance, conflict or missed opportunities to fulfil your mission.

Heal this karma by accepting people as they are, opening your mind, travelling and learning from diverse cultures, avoiding political disputes and debt, engaging in peaceful and service-oriented actions and releasing limiting inherited beliefs.

✷ ARCANA 22 ✷

Your ancestral karma is about supreme spiritual potential, freedom of the soul and self-actualization. You carry the energy to explore the world, expand your consciousness and transform inherited restrictions into liberation. When blocked, this can appear as fear, mental or emotional imprisonment, attachment or limiting beliefs.

Heal this karma by seeking freedom in thought and action, forgiving and accepting your ancestors, avoiding dishonesty or anything shady, travelling to expand your perspective, reinventing yourself when necessary and creating independent resources.

YOUR KARMIC GIFTS

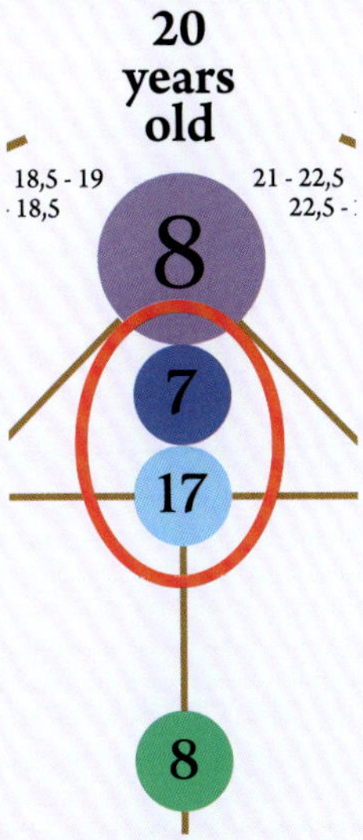

Your Karmic Gifts

✷ ARCANA 3 ✷

You possess creative skills from past lives, excelling in artistic expression and design. Your natural understanding of beauty and aesthetics reflects previous experiences in nurturing and guiding others. You provide emotional support and comfort to those around you and have a special gift for culinary creation that serves as a profound expression of love and connection. As your creative energy is released, you attract fulfilment and abundance, underpinned by a commitment to empowerment and justice.

✷ ARCANA 4 ✷

You possess strong past-life imprints tied to wealth creation and leadership, demonstrating natural skills in prosperity building and resource management. Instinctively commanding respect, you are adept at planning, negotiation and fostering long-term growth. Your resilience enables you to tackle challenges effectively, guided by practical wisdom and sharp financial instincts. To maximize your potential, embrace leadership confidently, inspire through clarity and remain flexible in collaboration, allowing your influence to grow while balancing strength with openness.

✷ ARCANA 5 ✷

You possess a profound spiritual and intellectual legacy from past lives, endowed with wisdom that transcends the material world. Naturally inclined to teach and guide, your soul is dedicated to learning and imparting truth. With a clear and logical mind, you analyse complex situations with precision. Effective communication is a key strength; your words resonate with clarity and charisma, making you a persuasive and enlightening presence for those seeking guidance. Your past experiences enhance your mentoring abilities, allowing you to lead through understanding rather than force.

✷ ARCANA 6 ✷

You have a profound past-life connection to beauty, harmony and human relationships. Your soul is attuned to enhancing environments through creative expressions like design and art. Your presence elevates your surroundings, reflecting a commitment to beauty. You naturally understand emotional dynamics, fostering harmony and making others feel valued. Additionally, your communication skills allow you to express ideas with clarity and charisma, enabling you to captivate and inspire others through storytelling and public speaking.

✷ ARCANA 7 ✷

You possess a strong divine imprint tied to entrepreneurship and inspired action, driven by confidence and optimism. Your quick, intuitive approach allows you to face challenges with resilience, transforming obstacles into progress. Notably, your ability to motivate and uplift others creates a positive environment, inspiring them to realize their potential. Your entrepreneurial spirit not only fosters personal success but also acts as a catalyst for growth in those around you.

✷ ARCANA 8 ✷

You possess a strong past-life imprint characterized by objective analysis, karmic understanding and higher law. Your clear, structured and methodical mind allows for precise perception of cause-and-effect patterns. You recognize the interconnectedness of events, choices and consequences, reflecting your experience in systems like law and philosophy. A key talent is guiding others through karmic insight and self-awareness, enhancing their understanding of their life path. You merge logic and intuition to support personal evolution, while having the potential for long-term stability and success through consistency and integrity.

✷ ARCANA 9 ✷

You have a significant past-life connection to teaching and the transmission of knowledge, marked by your ability to simplify complex concepts. Your investigative mind, fuelled by curiosity, seeks hidden truths across various subjects, including scientific and spiritual domains. Solitude aids your thinking, enabling meaningful discoveries. Your understanding transcends intellectual knowledge, bridging material and spiritual realms.

✷ ARCANA 10 ✷

You possess a powerful spiritual essence that enhances your creativity, intuition and inspired action. Your natural ability to generate original ideas attracts opportunities and abundance, reflecting a history of manifesting visions with clarity. Your intuition guides you in recognizing patterns and seizing possibilities, enabling you to bring innovative projects to fruition. Your unique energy and originality inspire others, while your communication skills foster trust and collaboration. Additionally, your optimistic, adventurous spirit propels you to explore new horizons, enriching your creative perspective.

✷ ARCANA 11 ✷

You possess a deep-rooted past-life imprint characterized by resilience, leadership and healing energy. This manifests as persistence and focus, enabling you to overcome challenges and inspire others through your enthusiasm and determination. Your healing abilities, whether expressed through touch or holistic practices, create balance and restoration for those around you, and your energy uplifts communities while fostering personal growth and transformation, positioning you as a natural guide or mentor.

✷ ARCANA 12 ✷

You possess a profound connection to creativity and empathy from past lives, allowing you to see the world uniquely. This perspective fosters imaginative ideas that inspire others through various mediums like art and writing. Your deep understanding of people's needs enhances the impact of your work, enabling you to uplift and mentor those around you. Past experiences have instilled in you a bold vision and a readiness to explore new ideas, helping you transform concepts into creations that resonate widely.

✷ ARCANA 13 ✷

You have a significant past-life imprint characterized by courage, adaptability and a transformative influence. You possess an innate ability to stay calm and decisive under pressure, reflecting past experiences that required bravery. Your tendency to initiate change and embrace risk inspires those around you. With an entrepreneurial spirit, you adapt to new circumstances and reveal depth in your actions. Your past lives have given you a deep understanding of transformation and the human experience, enabling you to support others through change and personal growth.

✷ ARCANA 14 ✷

You have a strong past-life imprint linked to healing, empathy and creativity, enabling you to restore balance and bring clarity to others. This is expressed in various fields such as art, music, writing and holistic healing. You intuitively sense the needs of others, crafting transformative experiences through creative expression and emotional support. Your spiritual energy enhances your ability to inspire and facilitate personal growth, while your past lives have nurtured your patience, sensitivity and intuition, enriching all that you create and share.

✷ ARCANA 15 ✷

You possess a powerful past-life imprint related to charisma, insight and a transformative influence, enabling you to perceive the truth in others and guide them authentically. Your exceptional communication skills and intuitive grasp of human dynamics reflect extensive experience in mentoring and spiritual guidance. You assist individuals in overcoming struggles and realizing their potential while fostering connection and motivation. Your abilities to charm, empathize and empower enable you to navigate social networks effectively and create collaborative, growth-oriented environments.

✷ ARCANA 16 ✷

You possess a strong past-life imprint linked to transformation and renewal, enabling you to release outdated structures while embracing new opportunities for growth. Your experiences foster resilience in the face of adversity, allowing you to assist others in overcoming limitations. This revolutionary spirit, cultivated through past lives, empowers you to inspire change and have a meaningful impact on both personal and collective levels.

✷ ARCANA 17 ✷

You possess a strong past-life imprint linked to charisma and creative influence, naturally attracting attention and inspiring others. With skills in performance and communication, you are able to captivate audiences and transform your talents into impactful opportunities. Your experiences in media, entertainment and mystical practices resonate with others, fostering connection and influence. Past lives have enhanced your showmanship, emotional awareness and persuasive communication skills, enabling you to leave a lasting impression.

✷ ARCANA 18 ✷

You have a profound past-life influence linked to creativity and spiritual insight, enabling you to rapidly manifest imaginative ideas. Your experiences in various artistic fields grant you a special connection to mystical energies, allowing for the perception of subtle dimensions. This background nurtures your intuitive abilities and openness to experimentation, empowering you to translate visions into impactful creations across multiple mediums, including writing, the visual arts and spiritual teaching, ultimately making a meaningful difference in creative and spiritual communities.

✷ ARCANA 19 ✷

You possess a powerful past-life imprint characterized by positivity and leadership, enabling you to create joyful experiences and inspire others. Your innate charisma and generosity foster deep connections, promoting trust and collaboration. Your strategic creativity attracts opportunities, making you a natural leader and guide, particularly in event planning, entertainment, marketing or coaching, where your skills converge to create memorable and impactful experiences.

✷ ARCANA 20 ✷

You possess a unique ability to connect with non-physical energies, offering insights into life and spirituality that others may overlook. Your extrasensory skills, combined with a clear-thinking approach, allow for profound understanding and learning from experiences. Strong family and ancestral ties contribute to your wisdom and intuition, enhancing your identity. By embracing your heritage, you refine your abilities and gain perspective beneficial to others. This makes you particularly suited for roles such as spiritual consultant, medium, tarot reader or coach, where your insights can facilitate transformation and positive change.

✷ ARCANA 21 ✷

You possess a remarkable ability for conflict resolution through empathy and patience. Your curiosity and openness to diverse perspectives enhance your adaptability and insight. Proficiency in languages and cultural awareness provide you with global opportunities to bridge differences effectively. By embracing your strengths and thinking boldly, you can inspire collaboration and foster harmony, making a significant impact in fields such as mediation, diplomacy and international relations.

✷ ARCANA 22 ✷

You possess a natural talent for adaptability and resilience, enabling you to handle challenges gracefully while maintaining freedom. Your thoughtful rather than reactive responses stand out as a key strength. You have a strong affinity with children, using your understanding to foster joy and meaningful learning. You excel in roles that blend creativity, organization and entertainment, including event planning, children's programmes, educational entrepreneurship, digital content creation and designing inspiring products and experiences.

YOUR KARMIC TASKS

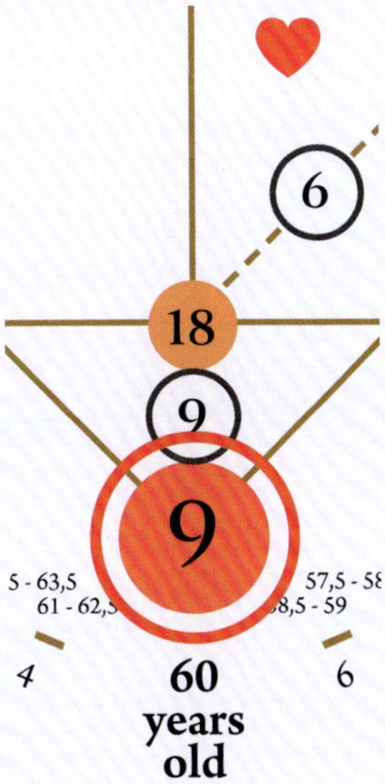

Your Karmic Tasks

✷ ARCANA 3 ✷

You carry a significant karmic theme related to feminine energy. Unresolved emotional patterns may lead to issues with control and neglecting emotional or spiritual needs. Healing involves being gentler with yourself and improving relationships with the feminine through emotional work or therapy. For those who more strongly resonate with masculine energy, balancing masculine drive with feminine sensitivity is essential, fostering independence, integrity and emotional maturity. Engaging in physical activities can also contribute to emotional grounding.

✷ ARCANA 4 ✷

You possess a karmic theme linked to masculine energy, particularly regarding fatherhood and authority. Your current life challenge is to balance strength with sensitivity, shifting from dominance to empathy. Healing relationships with father figures is vital. Professionally, pursue growth through fostering cooperative relationships. Spiritually, embrace your feminine energies by expressing your emotions and gratitude more often. If parenting, approach it with love and patience.

✷ ARCANA 5 ✷

You are grappling with a karmic lesson centred on spirituality, authority and familial roles. This life calls for a transformation of authority from control into wisdom, flexibility and tolerance. Embrace diverse perspectives, loosen control of family relationships and organize your thoughts and priorities to overcome judgemental tendencies.

✷ ARCANA 6 ✷

You are experiencing a karmic lesson focused on emotional healing related to love, self-worth and relationships. Past heartbreak and dependency may manifest as low self-esteem, so your current task is to build self-love, treat yourself kindly and stop seeking approval from others. Viewing relationships clearly without idealization will create space for genuine connections.

✷ ARCANA 7 ✷

You possess a karmic pattern related to ambition, reflecting past lives as a warrior or someone lacking direction. You may struggle to achieve success and experience self-doubt, and your current life lesson is to balance your inner strength with purpose, set clear goals, and adopt a consistent approach rather than a chaotic one. Trusting others and engaging in new experiences can help. Incorporating physical activities and a structured routine will aid in overcoming stagnation and doubt.

✷ ARCANA 8 ✷

You possess a heightened sensitivity to fairness, justice and integrity, which may lead to feelings of being wronged or misunderstood and result in grudges, conflicts and even legal disputes. The lesson for your soul in this lifetime is to move away from judgement and cultivate acceptance and maturity. Uphold honesty and responsibility, particularly in promises and in financial matters, and see challenges as lessons. Techniques such as meditation and mindful reflection can enhance emotional stability.

✷ ARCANA 9 ✷

You possess profound wisdom derived from past experiences, which you may have previously concealed due to fear or emotional withdrawal. In this lifetime, your challenge is to share this knowledge to guide and inspire others. While you may prefer solitude and introspection, you are encouraged to open up, share your truth and lead others through your insights.

✷ ARCANA 10 ✷

In this lifetime, you are facing challenges related to independence, self-direction and inner trust, and are learning to assert your identity. Previous lifetimes may have left you passive and overly influenced by others. This life encourages you to define your preferences and act on your impulses, despite possible struggles with procrastination and excessive worrying. Growth comes from trusting your intuitive rhythm, which fluctuates between motivation and quietude. Embracing travel and new experiences enriches your spirit, while financial responsibility and gratitude will align you with abundance.

✷ ARCANA 11 ✷

You possess a potent inner energy that requires careful direction. While it can create momentum when harnessed properly, it risks becoming overwhelming if ignored. Your growth involves breaking old cycles of force and applying your drive constructively. Engaging in strength-focused activities and allowing time for rest will help manage your intensity. Your primary lesson is to lead with patience, awareness and emotional intelligence while softening your approach through nature, meditation and sensitivity.

✷ ARCANA 12 ✷

You carry a karmic lesson highlighting the imbalance between selfishness and self-sacrifice. This may manifest as feelings of powerlessness, excessive responsibility for others or unwarranted guilt. The need to please can lead to low self-worth and emotional exhaustion. Healing involves reclaiming your value by setting limits, confidently pursuing what you deserve and engaging in creative expression to reconnect with your identity. It's crucial to charge fairly for your work, nurture yourself and maintain autonomy in relationships.

✷ ARCANA 13 ✷

You possess a karmic imprint linked to prior experiences of loss, change-induced fear and the avoidance of life's challenges, possibly from facing sudden death or situations evoking guilt and stagnation. These patterns may now manifest as anxiety about the future or an impulse to abruptly sever ties and start anew. Your mission in this lifetime is to fully embrace life, unencumbered by fear. So, release past burdens, declutter both physically and emotionally, and remain present in your actions. Engaging in practices such as yoga, meditation and stepping outside your comfort zone will enhance optimism and rekindle vitality. Choose growth over fear and embrace possibilities.

✷ ARCANA 14 ✷

You carry a karmic lesson focused on creativity, emotional balance and reconnecting with your soul. Past lives characterized by extremes such as addictions and material excess may have left you spiritually disconnected, leading to impulsiveness and emotional overload in this life. Your growth involves regulating your energy, slowing down and trusting natural outcomes. Embracing creativity as a meaningful pursuit and source of income is encouraged. Honesty and self-care are vital for building a healthier life structure. Water serves as a healing element, aiding emotional reset. Your lifetime task is to achieve balance, soften your ego and transform past excess into grounded creativity.

✷ ARCANA 15 ✷

You carry a karmic imprint related to shadow energy and the misuse of personal power, possibly reflecting struggles with jealousy and control in past lives. This manifests as irritability and a tendency to dominate when threatened. Your journey involves transforming these tendencies into awareness and compassion. Emotional flexibility, empathy and mindful communication are vital for healthier connections. Engaging in spiritual practices will help align you with your higher self, while avoiding manipulative behaviours and obsessive patterns can liberate you from karmic influences.

✷ ARCANA 16 ✷

You possess a strong karmic imprint associated with rebellion and transformation. This may manifest as inner restlessness and a cycle of breakdowns and rebuilds in your current life. Your mission includes facing challenges without blame or chaos, transforming destructive urges into conscious strength and maturity. Simplifying your lifestyle, practising discipline and engaging in mindful routines are essential for stabilizing your energy. Change should be welcomed, and acceptance of endings is vital for understanding life's transitions.

✷ ARCANA 17 ✷

You carry a karmic imprint influencing your visibility and ability to express your gifts, embodying a duality of seeking recognition and fearing exposure. This can result in creative stagnation. Your life lesson is to reclaim your inherent brilliance with humility and clarity, affirming your talents and integrating them with your purpose. Embrace your creative impulses, allowing any recognition to stem from authenticity and a desire to uplift others. Spiritually, reconnect with the Divine. This lifetime invites you to be a humble luminary, realizing your destined role without compromising your essence.

✷ ARCANA 18 ✷

You possess a karmic imprint linked to misuse of power and manipulation through magic, potentially causing anxiety and emotional imbalance in this life. This lifetime invites you to reclaim your intuitive power with integrity, dissolve old illusions and enhance your emotional stability through artistic expression and spiritual practices. The journey involves responsibly exploring esoteric knowledge and shifting your focus towards positivity, ultimately fostering healing and uplifting magic that benefits both yourself and others.

✷ ARCANA 19 ✷

You have a karmic lesson related to the responsible use of power and vitality. This lifetime calls for healing family-related wounds and transforming past aggressiveness into positivity. Your journey involves embracing joy, generosity and community engagement. By wisely distributing your energy and balancing ambition with kindness, you can fulfill your true strength and contribute positively to the world.

✷ ARCANA 20 ✷

You possess a karmic connection tied to family and ancestry. The echoes of past family conflicts may manifest as tension with relatives or an unclear purpose in this life. Signs of unresolved wounds include quick judgement of others and defensiveness towards change. Healing these patterns involves fostering healthier relationships and embracing forgiveness for your lineage and yourself. Transforming power into wisdom will enable you to understand rather than judge. Engaging in cleansing rituals and honouring your ancestors can help you clear emotional blockages and realign with your purpose.

✷ ARCANA 21 ✷

You carry a karmic imprint shaped by past conflicts and ideologies, often leading to defensiveness and mistrust of unfamiliar ideas. This lifetime's lesson involves embracing diversity and acting from peace and unity rather than fear and rigidity. Your journey includes becoming a global soul through travel, cultural engagement and compassionate leadership. You are encouraged to trust in the world, bridge differences and seek unity.

✷ ARCANA 22 ✷

You carry a karmic lesson focused on freedom and autonomy, shaped by past experiences of confinement or restrictive control. This may manifest as feeling trapped, overwhelmed or pressured, often leading to self-limitation and excessive responsibility. Your challenge is to reclaim freedom in all aspects of life by moving lightly, experimenting and allowing a natural flow instead of exerting control. Engaging in hobbies and routines will foster a sense of inner freedom, emphasizing that what truly belongs to you strengthens when allowed the space to really flourish.

CHAPTER 7

YOUR WELL-BEING

YOUR MATERIAL TASKS

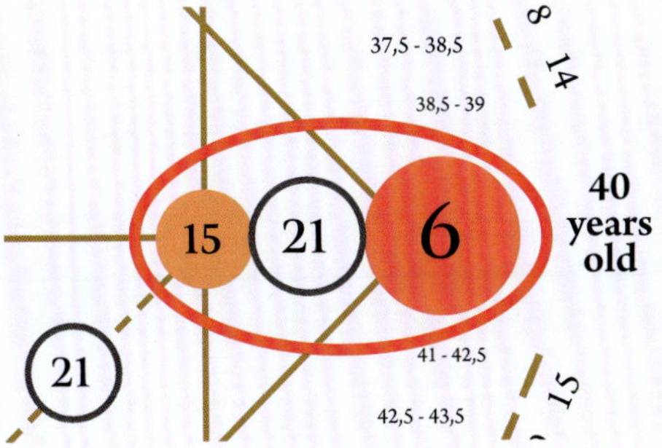

Your Material Tasks

The three energies in these positions reflect negative experiences related to money from your past incarnations. They highlight the factors that can lead to material difficulties in this life. Each reveals what must be worked through to ensure that financial challenges are not repeated. By addressing these karmic lessons, you can shift your relationship with money, overcome past limitations and create a more balanced and abundant financial experience. Unblocking material paths is also key to maintaining health and vitality and enjoying well-being in this life.

✷ ARCANA 2 ✷

Your financial success is linked to your relational skills, with empathetic instincts meeting others' needs. However, karmic memories of deception can negatively impact you, manifesting as financial instability and physical ailments if ignored. Issues with trust hinder clarity, leading to passivity, which is often mistaken for laziness. Healing involves embracing authenticity, fostering trust and focusing on suppressed emotions rather than blame. Embracing all emotions is essential for growth. Your health is also closely tied to your ancestral lineage, with unresolved family karmic patterns affecting your energy levels. Recognizing the aspects that need healing is crucial for balance. Your inner attitude, including honesty and acceptance, directly influences your well-being. Healing requires stillness and harmony. Returning to your inner centre can restore your energy when you are feeling unbalanced. Being out in nature will also play a vital role in restoring your equilibrium.

✷ ARCANA 3 ✷

Past experiences of self-sacrifice and the misuse of power can block your abundance and vitality. Overworking and neglecting self-care will weaken well-being, and strained relationships with women can hinder financial growth. Letting go of control and enjoying creativity will foster it. Practise generosity, care for your environment and prioritize self-care. Avoid routines and constant busyness. Grounding practices such as walking barefoot and connecting with nature are crucial for vitality. Your well-being relates to your maternal lineage and emotional family dynamics. Material wealth will emerge from a balance of masculine and feminine energies. Healthy relationships in general are key to unblocking your material well-being. Inner balance and time for rest and simple pleasures are also restorative.

✷ ARCANA 4 ✷

Past-life memories of the misuse of power may bring you resistance to success or fear of responsibility, leading to financial and physical challenges. Avoiding leadership roles or accountability will hinder your progress, while impatience will strain relationships. To prevent burnout, you should avoid trying to control every situation, embracing gratitude and patience instead. Healing involves compassionate leadership, softening rigid traits and accepting support, while still demonstrating responsible leadership and respect. To maintain physical strength and emotional balance, it's essential for you to cultivate a calm inner state, relinquish excessive control and ensure proper rest and movement. Engaging with nature through gardening and outdoor activities will enhance vitality, especially for those distanced from nature. Massage, gentle exercise and meditation are also beneficial. Acknowledging your ancestral lineage, particularly paternal influences, is vital for holistic healing and establishing family harmony.

✷ ARCANA 5 ✷

Issues from past lives, such as family betrayal, may lead to financial and physical instability. Clinging to rigid beliefs can also obstruct material flow. Your health will benefit from a structured routine that balances responsibility and rest, including physical movement, creativity and nature. Key factors for long-term vitality are self-care, proper nourishment and a consistent healing system. Maintaining respectful family connections enhances strength, and natural elements help well-being. Engaging with elders and resolving conflicts are essential for stability. Sharing knowledge and new experiences will promote growth and the healing of material karma.

✷ ARCANA 6 ✷

Unresolved past-life patterns around love, beauty and choice may be undermining your material stability and physical strength. Sacrificing authentic love for security, approval or appearances can block abundance and drain vitality. Your health will improve through self-acceptance, emotional honesty and balanced expression of sensual and creative energy. Long-term well-being is supported by healthy relationships, clear choices and respect for personal desires. Releasing perfectionism, fear of judgement and dependency will restore inner harmony. Surrounding yourself with beauty, nurturing sincere partnerships and spending joyful time in nature will strengthen your energy. Conscious communication, collaborative efforts and living in alignment with your heart will promote abundance and heal your material karma.

✷ ARCANA 7 ✷

Past-life gains through aggression may lead to dissatisfaction and stagnation in this life, and repeating such behaviours can create both financial and physical issues. To encourage abundance, approach life cooperatively, channel anger constructively and balance work with rest. Celebrate achievements, set structured goals and integrate leadership and collaboration, while avoiding isolation and laziness. Material success will result from clear goals and personal development in teamwork and leadership. You might consider balancing career goals with family life to maintain well-being. Your health will thrive with movement, early mornings and calming practices such as meditation and nature exposure. A positive mindset and caring for your physical foundation, particularly your joints and spine, are essential. Daily walks will foster clarity, strength and energy. Connection with nature, especially elements such as fire and earth, will enhance vitality, while water promotes relaxation.

✷ ARCANA 8 ✷

Past-life patterns related to material gain can lead to current-life imbalances, which must be recognized for healing. Emotional inflexibility will hinder your progress, so you should explore your motives, embrace flexibility and trust in a broader karmic rhythm. Honest financial practices and a re-evaluation of your childhood beliefs about money are necessary for healthier perspectives. Your health is best maintained through balance, with an emphasis on moderation. Early mornings, meditation and physical activity will restore vitality, while proximity to water will aid healing. Avoiding conflicts is essential, as they drain your energy and disrupt your harmony. Embracing peace and enjoying connection with nature will enhance your well-being, specifically through the elements of water and earth, while a positive outlook and an understanding of karma will foster prosperity.

✷ ARCANA 9 ✷

For you, the pursuit of knowledge should be approached with humility to avoid the misuse that drains vitality. Valuing personal abilities, maintaining social connections and looking after your physical health will enhance your energy and opportunities. Embracing inner wisdom will both aid self-healing and guide others, highlighting the importance of connecting depth with compassion and thought with spirit. In order for your health to thrive, it is crucial to disconnect from distractions and material pressures and engage with nature and quiet routines, meditation and gentle exercise. Solitude promotes personal care and balance, while letting go of resentment and fostering optimism benefits physical health.

✷ ARCANA 10 ✷

Stress and external expectations may disrupt your alignment with your true self, but embracing your inner guidance will foster a smoother journey. Disconnection from your goals due to overworking or passivity drains energy and resources; thus, clearly defining your desires and taking steps towards them is crucial. Gratitude, authenticity and joy enhance abundance, as do self-defined terms and flexible approaches, balancing striving with passivity. You can maintain optimal health by engaging in gentle movement, nurturing your mind and caring for your body. Key elements include restful sleep, fresh air, peaceful walks, a tidy environment and nourishing meals. Meditative practices and spiritual connections will contribute to balance, while cultivating trust in life's guidance will foster material stability and physical strength.

✷ ARCANA 11 ✷

Remember that true strength involves direction and intentional energy rather than dominance. Financial woes and impulsive choices can impact your material well-being, making structured routines and relaxation vital to prevent burnout. Balanced action will foster empowerment. Mindful management of aggression and the pursuit of meaningful goals will improve energy effectiveness, and trusting yourself without seeking external validation is crucial. Channelling strong emotions through sports and meditation aids your creative expression. Engaging in physical activity and nature positively impacts your health and well-being by bringing mental clarity, emotional balance and stress relief. Sports and walks help you reconnect with your inner strength and align your physical and spiritual energy.

✷ ARCANA 12 ✷

Your past experiences may be leading to self-sacrifice and emotional manipulation, draining your vitality. A powerless mindset and lack of boundaries may be undermining your self-worth. To grow, express your desires directly and recognize that your outer experiences reflect your inner state. Healing involves forgiving yourself and establishing boundaries. You can maintain good health through creativity and compassion for yourself. Your well-being will improve if you treat yourself with love, balancing your routine and nurturing yourself with practices like self-massage and visiting uplifting places. Embracing your uniqueness and focusing on your own well-being will strengthen you both physically and materially. Generosity flows from self-nourishment rather than depletion.

✷ ARCANA 13 ✷

Patterns of aggression and fear of change from past lifetimes may be hindering your current abundance by manifesting as stagnation and unhealthy habits. Embracing change, completing cycles and letting go of outdated beliefs are crucial for healing and prosperity. You will flourish with an active, nature-connected lifestyle that includes movement, fresh air and natural elements. Maintaining clean spaces and practising physical hygiene, along with pure foods, grounding exercises and breathwork, will enhance your vitality and clarity. For you, growth often results from significant transformations rather than gradual improvement, with crises acting as catalysts. Engaging in spiritual practices and connecting with supportive communities can help restore balance and protect against negative influences.

✷ ARCANA 14 ✷

Your past-life karmic patterns may manifest as financial or energetic blockages, self-doubt or the neglect of personal talents. Healing involves patience, gratitude, moderation and addressing any addictive behaviours while trusting your inner guidance. Techniques such as water therapy, meditation and forgiveness will strengthen your self-reliance and align spiritual with material growth. Your emotional health is intricately linked to your physical well-being, with calmness enhancing vitality and heaviness leading to tension. Rejuvenation can be achieved through gentle fasting, natural meals, cleansing, water therapies, herbal treatments, sauna rituals, steady sleep and other forms of self-care. Creative outlets such as art, music or writing will promote your emotional balance and strengthen your intuition. Additionally, meditation and energy practices will support both material stability and overall wellness. Embracing uncertainty and fostering compassion will lead to resilience and spiritual maturity, with authentic connections turning challenges into opportunities.

✷ ARCANA 15 ✷

Unhealthy financial pursuits in this life may stem from your past-life patterns, and ignoring these tendencies will disrupt your prosperity. Healing involves embracing all the aspects of yourself and using your insights to uplift others. Decluttering, addressing vices and cultivating ethical financial habits will promote stability. Clear communication of needs and disciplined resource management can transform your personal energy into abundance. Honouring your intuition and desires supports your well-being, while conscious restraint prevents destructive patterns from being expressed. Your well-being relies on maintaining a calm inner world, as strong emotions can deplete your vitality. Spiritual rituals, fasting, herbal treatments, exercise and mindful energy work will restore balance.

✷ ARCANA 16 ✷

Your past lifetimes may have involved sacrificing your inner growth for material comfort, leading to karmic effects, including self-sabotage. Stagnation, fear of change and resistance to growth can all be hindering your abundance. To restore momentum, cultivate small positive daily habits, embrace change, balance activity with rest and share insights. You will thrive through physical activity, spiritual practices and outdoor experiences, relying on clean spaces, a healthy diet and hydration for energy stability. Releasing control and old patterns enhances both vitality and prosperity, while nurturing sacred spaces and healthy rhythms can strengthen alignment. Abandoning outdated habits and clearing past energies can lead to both material and spiritual abundance.

✷ ARCANA 17 ✷

Your past lifetimes may have led to self-doubt and disconnection from your desires due to external pressures. Current patterns can also hinder financial flow and health if ignored. Abundance may be obstructed by pride or a belief in your superiority. Maintaining humility and embracing creativity are crucial for healing and self-expression amid challenges. You recharge by connecting with nature and earthly elements, finding peace in water, plants, animals and crystals. Creative expression, herbal practices and travel are essential for energy restoration. Trusting your intuition and recognizing subtle signs will foster growth.

✷ ARCANA 18 ✷

Past negative patterns, such as misguided energy work and fear-based beliefs, may be blocking your abundance and draining your energy. Your well-being is influenced by lunar rhythms and energies, with good sleep, clean water, gentle cleansing and mindful practices enhancing your health. Mastering your inner world through deliberate thought and emotional processing is essential for healing. Embracing your intuitive power will help restore your strength, while studying spirituality and psychology will activate wealth, guided by your ethical psychic sensitivity.

✷ ARCANA 19 ✷

For you, a positive mindset, joy and nurturing connections, particularly with family, will contribute to material abundance. However, past-life conflicts and negative patterns, influenced by impulsive behaviours or self-centred attitudes, can impede financial prosperity and health. Emotional clarity and helping others can restore balance. Embracing leadership and community involvement will foster growth, while nurturing your inner child and joyful interactions will further enhance your well-being. You thrive on generosity and connection and your body flourishes in space, sunlight and nature. Engaging in outdoor activities and practices like meditation will recharge your vitality.

✷ ARCANA 20 ✷

Your overall well-being is closely tied to your ancestral lineage and family relationships. Patterns of distancing, betrayal or shame can block prosperity. Deep exploration of your family history can alleviate resentment and open pathways, while forgiveness will dissolve inherited limitations. A clear and peaceful family connection will foster physical health and emotional balance, while chaos and conflicting opinions can hinder energy flow. Transforming limiting beliefs about money and embracing spiritual growth are essential for unlocking true potential and abundance.

✷ ARCANA 21 ✷

Your past-life issues can manifest in financial challenges and health problems; thus, patience, gratitude and steady effort are crucial for abundance. Resisting opportunities hampers growth, while openness to diverse perspectives and collaboration foster both material and spiritual development. Engaging in travel, service and actions that impact many aligns with your soul mission and promotes compassion and connectivity. To achieve material stability, it is essential to surpass old limits while respecting personal boundaries. Embracing self-acceptance, curiosity and diversity will invite greater support from life, while your health and vitality will improve with a clear inner light and strong spiritual connection through practices such as meditation, exploration and alignment with higher guidance, along with pure water, clean air, energy work and rest.

✷ ARCANA 22 ✷

Your past lives may have been marked by restriction or suppression, and such patterns impede abundance. Financial imbalances, whether hoarding or impulsive spending, also weaken material flow. To have a fulfilling work life, you need a balance between security and freedom, promoting the exploration of new opportunities, especially those that allow for creativity and flexibility. Detachment from attachments is also necessary; rigid schedules and controlling environments will hinder your growth. Learning to strike a balance between freedom and responsibility is vital, as is a lighthearted approach, for joy, curiosity and playfulness will foster prosperity. Pursue unconventional paths such as creative work or travel and embrace guiding others to joy and freedom through spiritual wisdom. For your health to thrive, it's important not to be limited by your parents' patterns or restrictions. Instead, prioritize self-care, stay physically active and consciously choose your own healthy path. For you, true abundance is found in cultivating mental, emotional, creative, financial and spiritual freedom.

THE CHAKRAS AND YOUR HEALTH MAP

Your health map (as pictured on page 15) is derived directly from the Destiny Matrix chart itself. The numbers shown on the Matrix correspond to the chakras and are colour-coded to match each energy centre. When you are calculating the health and chakra map, most numbers are formed by combining the two numbers that share the same colour in the chart (i.e. two chart positions). The exception is the Manipura chakra; there is only one yellow chart position, so in this case, the value is added to itself (e.g. 9 + 9 = 18).

In this map, the physical aspects of health ('physics') are read through the Earth line, while energetic vitality ('energy') is reflected in the sky line. Emotional health ('emotions') emerges from the interaction of these two forces, where physical structure and energetic flow meet.

✷ ARCANA 1 ✷

Muladhara: Strong individuality, power, high energy, confidence, will, creativity, fearlessness. Many opportunities for a successful life. No major health issues.

Svadhisthana: Strong sexual appeal and desire, sexual freedom, bodily confidence, dominance in relationships. Self-sufficient, often changes partners. Unique, creatively gifted, strong reproductive health. A natural introvert who needs no one to feel complete.

Manipura: A powerful, talented, confident achiever. Total control over own destiny. A natural leader who stops at nothing to win and enjoys success.

Anahata: Strong charisma, easily wins and controls others. Emotionally untouchable, deeply self-centred. Popular and socially skilled, but has a tendency to be selfish within their relationships.

Vishuddha: Persuasive, eloquent, independent thinker. Influences others through speech and communication. A visible, influential social figure.

Ajna: Ambitious, creative, highly intelligent, goal-driven. Achieves a great deal and earns respect. Relies on logic over intuition; nothing is done impulsively.

Sahasrara: Vast ambition and potential. Strong influence on reality, high creativity. Success in all pursuits. Highly open and receptive, able to channel energy into chosen areas.

Result: Your condition improves with clear goals, good rest, healthy boundaries and self-care, and worsens with overwork, poor priorities, bad sleep, unstable habits and ignoring health needs.

✷ ARCANA 2 ✷

Muladhara: Natural worldly wisdom, adaptability, insight. Cunning, secretive, dual in nature. Completely closed off, private, avoids self-disclosure. Prefers observing and listening. Weak health; possible alcohol attraction.

Svadhisthana: Emotional and sexual coldness, passivity. Frequent loneliness. Possible kidney and reproductive issues.

Manipura: Ability to store energy and knowledge. Introverted, detached, passive, intuitive, magically inclined. Deep inner balance. Needs partnership. Saves money rather than invests.

Anahata: Emotionally distant and hard to approach. Keeps feelings hidden.

Vishuddha: Restrained, quiet, hidden ambitions. Fear of public speaking. Poor at audience interaction. Self-expression through knowledge or occult work. Speaks rarely, but precisely and painfully accurately, targeting weaknesses.

Ajna: Powerful, well-developed intuition used skillfully. Access to knowledge others lack.

Sahasrara: Intuition reaching divine revelation. A life guided by higher wisdom.

Result: Your condition improves with inner balance, self-care, intuition and letting go of control, and worsens with emotional instability, dishonesty, gossip, overbearing environments and avoiding difficult situations.

✷ ARCANA 3 ✷

Muladhara: Strong health, closeness to nature, creativity, fertility, independence, self-reliance.

Svadhisthana: Fertility, persistence, initiative and creative results. Pleasure for self and partner.

Manipura: Independence, self-sufficiency, strong maternal instinct, life satisfaction, focus on the family.

Anahata: Kind, caring, responsive, nature-oriented. Radiates calm and confidence. A loyal partner brings fulfilment and unconditional love.

Vishuddha: Bright, creative, gently persuasive. Caring, helpful, often in a leadership role. A confident speaker, comfortable in public, enjoys attention.

Ajna: Strong creative drive and appreciation of beauty.

Sahasrara: Energy that brings grounding.

Result: Your condition improves with self-care, love, comfort, nature and nurturing connections, and worsens with emotional coldness, impatience, pride, overfocus on work or money and neglecting personal well-being.

✷ ARCANA 4 ✷

Muladhara: Strong life-force and physical stamina. Home-oriented, traditional, reliable family person. Tendency to be impulsive, sharp, demanding, strict.

Svadhisthana: Family-centred, values home and stability. Dominant within the family, tends to control others.

Manipura: Solid health and material stability. Reason over emotion; feelings suppressed. Ambitious, power-driven, ready to step over others to lead.

Anahata: Strong, power-seeking personality. Hides emotions to avoid the appearance of weakness. Appears cold but is actually controlled and restrained.

Vishuddha: A natural manager and leader. Reaches a high status, has authority. Commanding speech; rigid mindset with no tolerance for opposing views.
Ajna: Strict logic and analytical thinking. Trusts only facts and personal knowledge. Decisive, inflexible, sceptical. Successful leader. Career-driven. Poor intuition, only intellect and reason.
Sahasrara: Clear value system and mental sobriety. Acts deliberately, fully aware of choices.
Result: Your condition improves with rest, balance, healthy relationships, regular checkups and moderate activity, and worsens with overwork, conflict, excessive control, constant stress and physical overexertion.

✷ ARCANA 5 ✷

Muladhara: A will to live that is shaped by spiritual needs.
Svadhisthana: Low sexual drive, focus on spirituality. Capable of selfless love, loyal and faithful to a partner.
Manipura: Emotional, sensitive, deeply devoted. Guided by faith; spiritual matters outweigh material ones. Values hierarchy, works for purpose and self-realization rather than money.
Anahata: Heart-centred, highly sensitive and vulnerable. Needs emotional support. Tends to teach life lessons. Clear moral boundaries, sincere faith, love of spirituality.
Vishuddha: Pleasant, warm and easy to communicate with.
Ajna: Guided by ethics and morality. Often drawn to music, spiritual guidance, religion or mysticism.
Sahasrara: Ability to form an ideology rooted in high morals and ethics. Often linked to religion, science or strong oratory skills.
Result: Your condition improves with healthy eating, regular checkups, mindful care and spiritual balance, and worsens with self-medication, lack of faith, family conflict and inner unrest.

✷ ARCANA 6 ✷

Muladhara: Tendency to fall in love easily, low energy reserve. Constant self-doubt and uncertainty in all areas of life.
Svadhisthana: Insecurity about attractiveness. Strong attraction, but weak embodiment of sexual energy. Possible fear of intimacy or frequent partner changes.
Manipura: Warm emotions, romantic nature, indecision. Strong need to love and be loved.
Anahata: Life revolves around love and partnership. Easily tempted, unstable relationships, love triangles. Constant doubt and concern over other people's opinions. Struggles to be alone.
Vishuddha: Seeks harmony, tactful, friendly, compliant. Expressive speaker but highly dependent on others' opinions; true thoughts remain hidden.
Ajna: Love as the main life value. Kind, trusting, unsure of self, struggles with decisions.
Sahasrara: Relationship ethics are central. Strives for harmony, wholeness and deep psychological understanding.
Result: Your condition improves with self-acceptance, emotional balance, movement and seeking support when needed, and worsens with

self-criticism, inactivity, isolation, unhealthy behaviours and neglecting health care.

✷ ARCANA 7 ✷

Muladhara: Immense inner power, strong health, high endurance. Loves sports, competition, extremes, travel. In the worst case, aggression, periods of deep emotional struggle.
Svadhisthana: Strong sexual energy, assertive, free of complexes. Seeks new experiences. Negative aspect: instability.
Manipura: Huge vitality, active and freedom-loving. Direct, rough, impulsive, often goes too far. Follows own path, highly ambitious, stubborn, aggressive, goal-driven, achieves success.
Anahata: Clear about desires, fearless risk-taker. Passionate, adventurous, loves life and sport. Extreme egoist, lives for self-interest.
Vishuddha: Active, independent, freedom-seeking, stands out. Fun and humorous but can be considered rude. Strong speaking skills.
Ajna: Strong self-belief, flexible and fast thinker. Creative, decisive. Life is seen as a constant struggle. Intuition and logic are both strong.
Sahasrara: Driven by intense self-expression and the need to stand out. A life of constant change and struggle. In the worst case, aggression and chaos.

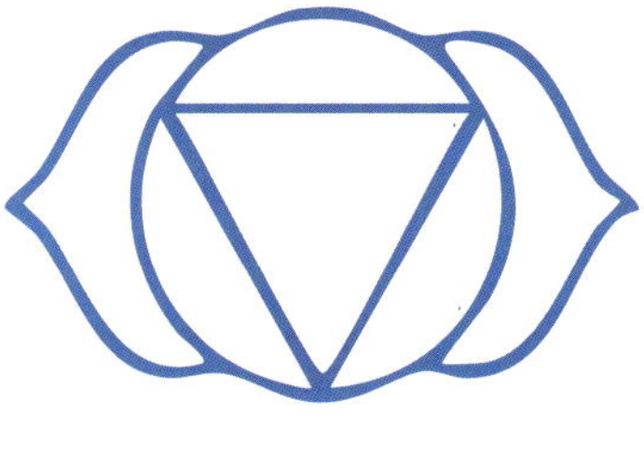

Result: Your condition improves with an active, disciplined, healthy lifestyle and regular checkups, and worsens with laziness, loss of self-control, overwork, risky behaviour and neglecting health.

✷ ARCANA 8 ✷

Muladhara: Ancestral burden that is shaped by inherited patterns and parental scripts. Restriction, conformity, inferiority complex, a desire to live by the rules.
Svadhisthana: Sexual suppression.
Manipura: Goal-oriented through honest means. Strong drive for justice. Often linked to law and order or government work.
Anahata: Heightened sense of justice. Even minor injustice causes deep pain, leading to emotional closure and the inability to give or receive love.
Vishuddha: Restrained self-expression, cautious and distrustful. Selective with people. Honest, principled, never insincere.
Ajna: Excessive self-control. Has difficulty accepting ideas outside a familiar worldview.
Sahasrara: Life feels meaningful; satisfaction with personal achievements.
Result: Your condition improves with honesty, following medical advice, balanced routines, healthy eating, exercise and calmness, and worsens with dishonesty, overwork, emotional instability, a lack of structure and ignoring health.

✷ ARCANA 9 ✷

Muladhara: Self-focused, egocentric, stingy. Struggles to open up in partnership. Comfortable alone, even among others, feeling separate.

Svadhisthana: Sexual complexes. Can co-exist with a partner yet remain emotionally distant.

Manipura: Low energy but high endurance. Persistent loneliness, emotional restraint, inner detachment.

Anahata: Hides feelings, shows little affection despite deep passion. Extremely loyal and devoted. In the worst case, suppresses emotions and rejects attachments, while holding deep unexpressed love for the world.

Vishuddha: Reserved, private, avoids self-display. Inner freedom. Speaks rarely, briefly and only on meaningful topics.

Ajna: Egocentric, spiritually focused, intelligent but closed off. Difficulty presenting self. In the worst case, excessive introversion, poor expression, weak memory, vision issues.

Sahasrara: Source of wisdom. Independent spirit, unwilling to submit.

Result: Your condition improves with self-care, spiritual and physical practices, rest, social balance and healthy habits, and worsens with isolation, inactivity, poor sleep, anxiety and neglecting health.

✷ ARCANA 10 ✷

Muladhara: Fortune can both reward and deceive.

Svadhisthana: In the worst case, many short-lived romances or emotional suppression.

Manipura: Reliance on fate. Acts by mood, lacks clear goals, hopes for luck and often gets it.

Anahata: Uncertain in love, behaviour shifts with circumstances. Loves travel.

Vishuddha: Changeable personality; actions depend on mood and environment.

Ajna: Trusts fate more than self. Strong intellect, often technical. In the worst case, dizziness and blood pressure swings.

Sahasrara: Fatalistic worldview.

Result: Your condition improves with health care, calmness, positivity and following medical advice, and worsens with laziness, negativity, inconsistency in treatment, risky behaviour and ignoring health.

✷ ARCANA 11 ✷

Muladhara: Strong regenerative ability, self-healing, passion, deep need for love.

Svadhisthana: Attractiveness and passion, with control over desires. Turbulent personal life; in the worst case, driven by instincts.

Manipura: Passionate, kind, friendly. Short-tempered, dominant, manipulative.

Anahata: Intense passion; capable of deep love and strong hatred. Caring, protective of the weak.

Vishuddha: Warm, friendly, persuasive. Avoids conflict but can wound with words.

Ajna: Positive outlook, sharp intellect. Strategic, analytical, a quick problem-solver.

Sahasrara: Passionate yet gentle when influencing others.
Result: Your condition improves with exercise, rest, self-care, healthy habits and spiritual balance, and worsens with neglect, overstrain, inactivity, emotional stress and ignoring personal growth.

✷ ARCANA 12 ✷

Muladhara: Possible hereditary illnesses. Common issues include blood pressure, spine and leg disorders and strong sensitivity to environmental conditions. A healthy lifestyle, mindful diet, and balanced work–rest routine are important. Self-doubt, anxiety, masochism, endurance of hardship and acceptance of a personal burden.
Svadhisthana: Sexual insecurities, dissatisfaction with self. Non-traditional view of family.
Manipura: Passive outlook on life, masochism, guilt, dissatisfaction with self and life, the avoidance of responsibility. In a positive form, self-sacrifice for a cause, often art or creativity.
Anahata: Vulnerability to the world, learned helplessness, difficulty with self-defence. Resentment and constant need for approval. Failures form complexes, leading to bitterness towards others. Risk of cardiovascular issues.
Vishuddha: Behaviour may appear unusual to others. In severe cases, passivity, surrender to fate and inner restlessness. Possible throat and thyroid disorders, speech issues, neurodivergence.
Ajna: Inverted, unconventional perception of reality.
Sahasrara: Self-sacrifice and dependence on people or circumstances. At times, life in a 'golden cage'.
Result: Your condition improves with self-care, confidence, healthy routines, helping others, creativity and time in nature, and worsens with overwork, stress, bad habits, neglecting health and a lack of self-love.

✷ ARCANA 13 ✷

Muladhara: Strong survival instinct, ability to recover and adapt quickly. Life marked by frequent crises.
Svadhisthana: Frequent partner changes, instability in personal life, emotional sensitivity. Possible infertility or reproductive system disorders.
Manipura: Clear goals and relentless pursuit of them. Strong drive for power.
Anahata: Blunted sensitivity, difficulty expressing emotions or empathizing. Calm acceptance of events. In extreme cases, coldness, indifference, cruelty.
Vishuddha: Little concern for others' opinions. Sharp, sarcastic, provocative, prone to conflict and threats.
Ajna: Fragile psyche, yet resilient after breakdowns. High intellect, sharp speech, reason dominates emotion.

Sahasrara: Life filled with crises and unexpected events. Constant inner tension and anticipation of misfortune.
Result: Your condition improves with embracing change, spiritual growth, activity, travel and regular health care, and worsens with resistance to change, stress, overwork, low confidence and neglecting health.

✷ ARCANA 14 ✷

Muladhara: Limited but efficiently managed energy. Prolonged illnesses due to weak self-healing. Slow recovery.
Svadhisthana: Emotional stability, good stress tolerance, ability to maintain balance.
Manipura: Calm temperament, resilience, ability to smooth conflicts. Life's challenges are taken lightly. In the negative, inactivity, slowness, conservatism, a focus on comfort.
Anahata: Mental stability, loyalty, emotional introversion.
Vishuddha: Gentle communication, strong negotiation skills, peaceful conflict resolution.
Ajna: Psychologically healthy, average abilities. Conventional thinking, limited awareness, adherence to social norms.
Sahasrara: Contentment with little. Primary needs are basic human values: understanding, emotional warmth and support.
Result: Your condition improves with moderation, balance, patience, emotional control and creative or calming activities, and worsens with overwork, imbalance, laziness, emotional suppression and unhealthy habits.

✷ ARCANA 15 ✷

Muladhara: Inclination towards harmful habits leading to health decline. Ambition and the pursuit of money, fame and power, or conversely, low self-worth and withdrawal from worldly life.
Svadhisthana: Pleasure-seeking, indulgence in weaknesses, addictions.
Manipura: Self-deception that also misleads others. In extreme cases, addictions and an obsessive desire for wealth, or fear of material possessions.
Anahata: Self-interest dominates relationships; connections are formed for personal gain. In love, manipulation, seduction, passion.
Vishuddha: Strong eloquence and self-presentation skills, paired with deceit.
Ajna: Self-centred focus on rapid achievement by any means, obscuring the true perception of reality.
Sahasrara: Creative or applied talents. Ambition, risk-taking, adventurism, a drive for power.
Result: Your condition improves by avoiding bad habits, staying active, thinking positively and maintaining healthy relationships, and worsens with negative influences, indulgence and a lack of moderation.

✷ ARCANA 16 ✷

Muladhara: Adverse family environment with authoritarian suppression, leading to a difficult life path. High but destructive energy, expressed through self-harm or causing chaos and harm to others.

Svadhisthana: Strong sexual energy.

Manipura: Lack of self-control and direction. A chaotic life. Stress, anger, fear, self-destructive tendencies.

Anahata: Hatred towards self and others. The inability to form deep emotional bonds.

Vishuddha: Attention-seeking through conflict, arguments and fights. In severe cases, throat and thyroid issues.

Ajna: A narrow worldview, rejection of the unfamiliar. Irritability, aggression, hysteria, neuroses, manic-depressive states.

Sahasrara: In extreme cases, imbalance may manifest as headaches, nervous-system strain, or disturbances in mental clarity.

Result: Your condition improves with regular health care, calmness, optimism and preventive care, and worsens with fear, neglect, distrust of doctors and harmful habits.

✷ ARCANA 17 ✷

Muladhara: Detachment from worldly matters, focus on higher realms. Idealism may lead to remaining single.

Svadhisthana: Search for elevated relationships, an ideal, the pursuit of a guiding star. High potential with equally high demands, not always fulfilled. At times, virginity or possible infertility.

Manipura: More dreaming than acting, orientation towards the future.

Anahata: Loyalty, devotion, emphasis on spiritual love.

Vishuddha: Kindness and elevated social standing.

Ajna: Clear thinking, the ability to set goals and to assess situations accurately. High self-worth and demanding standards for self and others.

Sahasrara: Strong connection with higher forces, lofty ideals and elevated aspirations.

Result: Your condition improves with clear health plans, self-belief, activity, positivity and joyful rest, and worsens with despair, complaints, hiding or neglecting symptoms and ignoring treatment.

✷ ARCANA 18 ✷

Muladhara: Can cause addiction, possible mental disorders, fears, phobias and self-doubt. Unstable, unreliable and easily influenced.

Svadhisthana: Fearful, inconsistent, unsure of desires, confused in relationships and dissatisfied with personal life.

Manipura: Strong sensitivity to outside influences leads to emotional instability and fear of life. Struggles to choose and lives by trial and error.

Anahata: Heightened sensitivity combined with emotional coldness and insincerity. Resentment, imagined fears and distorted perception of reality.

Vishuddha: Low self-confidence, fear of communication, introversion, emotional instability. Difficulty fitting into society, unclear speech

and trouble expressing thoughts. In extreme cases, dishonesty and distortion of facts.
Ajna: Lack of self-confidence, fear of the future and poor understanding of events, leading to anxiety and constant tension. Reactions are driven mainly by emotions.
Sahasrara: Strong sensitivity and fantastic intuition.
Result: Your condition improves with positivity, self-confidence, spiritual growth, healthy habits and listening to your body, and worsens with fear, complaints, harmful habits and neglecting health.

✷ ARCANA 19 ✷

Muladhara: Strong vitality, good health, active creativity, love of life, strong ego. Fertility.
Svadhisthana: High sexual energy, vivid emotions, a need for family life. Children. Creativity.
Manipura: Clear goals, strong drive to achieve them, enjoyment of life.
Anahata: Openness, trust, sociability, kindness. Pleasant to be around, attracts attention and love. Love for children, family and life.
Vishuddha: Bright, talented, cheerful personality who demands respect and rejects minor roles.
Ajna: Realistic perception and creative talent.
Sahasrara: Inner harmony, life feels clear and comfortable.
Result: Your condition improves with order, planning, gratitude, spiritual practice, healthy relationships, hobbies and light activity, and worsens with overwork, negativity, arrogance, poor nutrition and lack of sunlight.

✷ ARCANA 20 ✷

Muladhara: Restless, action-driven, with strong energy for all pursuits.
Svadhisthana: Possible kidney and reproductive issues and an ongoing dissatisfaction in relationships.
Manipura: Strong career focus, drive for achievement and clear division between allies and opponents, good and evil.
Anahata: A strong sense of higher justice, the ability to discern truth and rare mistakes in choosing people and partners.
Vishuddha: Skill in leadership, motivation and clear, effective communication.
Ajna: Possible clairvoyant abilities and career orientation.
Sahasrara: Possible past-life memories, insights and contact with parallel worlds.
Result: Your condition improves with strong family ties, self-care, good sleep, proper nutrition and moderate activity, and worsens with family conflict, negative thinking, constant stress and neglecting health.

✷ ARCANA 21 ✷

Muladhara: Limitless opportunities in all areas. Large family. Relocation.

Svadhisthana: Great opportunities, no sexual blocks or prejudices. Fertility.

Manipura: Strong inner harmony.

Anahata: Self-sufficiency and inner peace. Harmony with self and others, unity with the world, no attachments or resentments.

Vishuddha: Ability to negotiate with anyone without limits. Active communication and travel.

Ajna: Harmony with self and the world, ability to understand and accept much.

Sahasrara: Vast possibilities and access to higher achievements.

Result: Your condition improves with personal principles, peace, tolerance, modern treatment and travel, and worsens with avoidance, outdated methods, fear and unwillingness to act or explore.

✷ ARCANA 22 ✷

Muladhara: Foolish, changeable, easily excitable and unstable. Good survival skills.

Svadhisthana: Has difficulty forming relationships, excessive openness, emotional sensitivity.

Manipura: Constantly changing activities without direction. Weak-willed, irresponsible, living only for the present.

Anahata: Simple, open, vulnerable and naive. Unable to love, seeking love like a child, without malice or resentment.

Vishuddha: Excessive talkativeness. Humour.

Ajna: Creatively gifted and internally free. At times, possible mental disorders and bad habits.

Sahasrara: Life instability, restlessness, impulsive actions. Strong connection with higher planes.

Result: Your condition improves with freedom, order, travel, outdoor activity, pets and creativity, and worsens with carelessness, bad habits, reckless behaviour and neglecting treatment.

CHAPTER 8

YOUR PATH TO LOVE

YOUR RELATIONSHIP CHANNEL

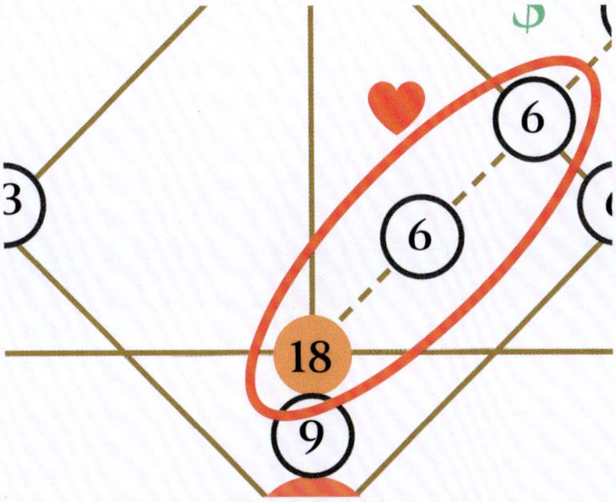

Your Relationship Channel

Your relationship channel represents the invisible path through which your interpersonal energy flows. It encompasses not only romantic relationships, but also interactions with others in all aspects of life: personal connections, business relationships and even casual encounters. It provides insight into your communication style, the types of people you attract and what you experience through these interactions.

YOUR LOVE BLOCKS

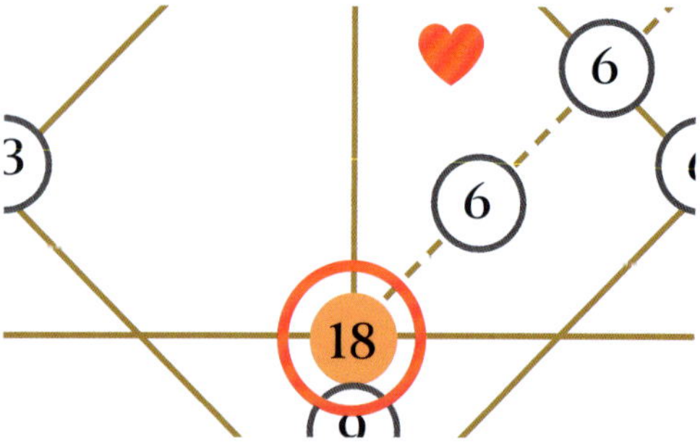

Your Love Blocks

✷ ARCANA 3 ✷

You might have a strong need to control everything. This leads to tension, impatience and mistrust, causing you to rely only on yourself and refuse help or support, which can drive love away. This need for control often results in a craving for recognition and excessive concern over material status, success, finances and personal image, causing you to neglect warmth and gratitude. Relationships can be complicated, oscillating between obsession and rejection. Feelings of withdrawal and a lack of fulfilment may arise, and personal traits may be mirrored back to you in your intimate relationships or exaggerated by those around you, prompting a necessary transformation. Personal growth emerges by loosening control, learning to trust and collaborate and allowing vulnerability.

✷ ARCANA 4 ✷

You may struggle with trust and adaptability, and overpower relationships through criticism, pride, control and competition. Issues with authority and money and a desire to be right can result in carrying burdens alone and neglecting personal needs. This need to control may block intimacy and lead to tension in your relationships. You may also fluctuate between dominance and control and overwhelm and withdrawal. Growth will come from releasing the need for rigid control and restoring harmony in your personal relationships by allowing cooperation and emotional openness.

✷ ARCANA 5 ✷

You may hinder love in relationships if pride and a desire for control dominate your perspective. This mindset leads to dismissing differing opinions, adhering strictly to rules and resisting flexibility, resulting in conflict. Factors such as fear of responsibility, societal pressures and unresolved issues with authority figures will exacerbate this rigidity, making closeness difficult. To improve relationships, it's essential to let go of the need for control, adjust your expectations and accept varying truths.

✷ ARCANA 6 ✷

You struggle in love when you lack self-value, dwell on the past and idealize others. This results in risky commitments, heavy choices and an aversion to responsibility. You may prioritize appearance and seek validation while doubting your feelings. This internal conflict between desiring intense emotions and fearing closeness can lead to boredom, drama or difficulty in sustaining long-term relationships. Jealousy, impulsiveness and a dependency on others' opinions intertwine with high expectations and self-doubt. Eventually, rejecting your true self prevents you from achieving the warmth and trust you seek, necessitating a shift towards self-acceptance and presence.

✷ ARCANA 7 ✷

You create distance in relationships by treating them as competitions rather than partnerships, which fosters conflict and dissatisfaction. This behaviour often stems from feelings of superiority, leading to stagnation and the avoidance of accountability. While you may try to win love through work and accomplishments, emotional coldness and self-doubt may persist. Jealousy and distrust can hinder commitment to your decisions, and choosing partners based on status or ego instead of genuine connection will perpetuate this cycle. To transform relationships into peaceful partnerships, it's essential to embrace vulnerability, clarify intentions and promote mutual respect.

✷ ARCANA 8 ✷

You hinder emotional closeness by treating relationships like a courtroom, where you impose judgements and demand compliance. This leads to anger, resentment and a focus on flaws rather than strengths. By clinging to past grievances and refusing to change, you perpetuate cycles of pain and mistake vulnerability for weakness. Fear of change and judgement stifles emotional warmth and intimacy, leaving you feeling empty despite an outwardly correct life. Trust must replace control, and emotional honesty must prevail over rigid rules for relationships to thrive and feel fulfilling.

✷ ARCANA 9 ✷

You isolate yourself by pushing away connections and closing yourself off from people, leading to heightened anxiety and self-criticism. This drains your energy and leaves little room for love or joy. Neglecting personal well-being and swinging to extremes in health and cleanliness fosters distance instead of safety. Pride and coldness lead to hidden emotions, feelings of superiority and withdrawal from social interactions. Without balance and openness, your relationships will remain unfulfilling and marked by loneliness.

✷ ARCANA 10 ✷

For you, struggling in relationships often stems from drifting through life and neglecting your true desires. Choosing incompatible partners and failing to engage meaningfully can create tension and disconnection. An overloaded schedule and emotional withdrawal will hinder genuine connection, while living on autopilot will lead to repeated mistakes. Distrust, impatience and ignoring intuition all create barriers to intimacy. Clinging to past experiences obstructs progress in the present, while imbalances in priorities drain emotional fulfilment. Relationships should embody joy and vitality, otherwise they lose significance. Remember that dissatisfaction indicates that personal transformation is necessary.

✷ ARCANA 11 ✷

Your fear of losing control and pursuit of dominance can push love away, creating emotional tension that manifests as irritability and conflict. You may oscillate between extremes in relationships, leading to mistrust and the avoidance of emotional intimacy. Workaholism and the neglect of personal needs can exacerbate these issues, making relaxation feel like weakness. A defensive attitude towards feedback and imbalanced responsibilities can exhaust your partner. To improve relationships, you must soften control, foster trust and embrace balance and rest.

✷ ARCANA 12 ✷

In your relationships, struggles arise when you neglect self-worth in favour of sacrifice and emotional merging, which can lead to a suffocating dynamic for both partners. Adopting a victim mentality and focusing on pain attracts negativity, suppresses personal growth and prevents new beginnings. Your tendency to solve others' problems and fear of letting go of unfulfilling situations perpetuates dependency and weak boundaries. This stagnation in relationships can persist until self-respect and strength take precedence over self-sacrifice, transforming closeness into a nourishing experience instead of a burdensome one.

✷ ARCANA 13 ✷

To maintain healthy relationships, it's essential to avoid allowing past experiences to dominate the present. Clinging to former attachments and fearing the future can alienate your partner. Unpredictability, viewing your partner as competition and a refusal to assume responsibility can also hinder trust and intimacy. Additionally, control issues, perfectionism, cynicism and excessive attachment can create an environment of discomfort and stagnation. The release of past burdens and a willingness to embrace change are necessary to achieve more fulfilling relationships.

✷ ARCANA 14 ✷

You may encounter difficulties in relationships due to indecision, a lack of self-control and extremes in behaviour. Issues such as fear of vulnerability, self-doubt and overthinking hinder intimacy. Mood swings and unresolved emotional burdens may also contribute to relationship tension, while an imbalance in giving and taking can exacerbate disconnection. Neglecting personal well-being through poor habits or addictions, as well as relying solely on logic or emotion, can further alienate love. Inner conflicts, such as desiring connection yet fearing commitment, create additional barriers. To build satisfying relationships, developing stability, trust and emotional balance is essential.

✷ ARCANA 15 ✷

You encounter challenges in love when control, aggression and dependence prevail. Attempts to manipulate or provoke your partner can drive them away, while prioritizing superficial pleasures hinders intimacy. Viewing people as objects and obsessively pursuing desires traps you in unhealthy patterns. Negative traits such as pride, envy and judgement generate tension, while co-dependency and unethical behaviour exacerbate conflict. Aggression and poor judgement both lead to unstable relationships. True love requires replacing obsession with self-awareness, respect and emotional balance.

✷ ARCANA 16 ✷

You may struggle in relationships due to aggression, emotional instability and a tendency towards destructiveness. Clinging to the past, fearing commitment or pursuing unhealthy partners impedes the development of healthy connections. Controlling behaviours, impulsive communication and rigid thinking can lead to conflicts and the deterioration of relationships. Additionally, pride, negativity and a persistent focus on flaws will hinder intimacy, while seeking external validation detracts from self-confidence. The inability to let go of resentment and the refusal to grow emotionally can trap you in conflict cycles. True love requires replacing destructive patterns with flexibility, self-trust and emotional maturity.

✷ ARCANA 17 ✷

For you, struggles in relationships often stem from dependence, insecurity or pride, which can cause issues such as excessive control or a sense of superiority. Emotional instability and detachment will hinder intimacy, while hiding your true self and having unrealistic expectations will only lead to disappointment. Past betrayals and fear of rejection may complicate trust, resulting in relationships that feel heavy and joyless. Then a lack of support and inspiration will replace warmth and playfulness, leaving love unfulfilling. Cultivate self-understanding, authenticity and emotional openness to nurture relationships.

✷ ARCANA 18 ✷

Challenges in love arise when fear, negativity and withdrawal influence your behaviour. Constant suspicion and projecting your fears can alienate your partner. Hiding your true self and engaging in manipulative behaviours will hinder trust and closeness. Emotional instability may be exacerbated by mood swings, anxiety and low self-esteem, fostering feelings of isolation. Strong maternal attachments and unresolved childhood issues may lead to dependence and fear of intimacy. Until you face your fears, accept your authentic self and open emotionally, your relationships will remain tense, distant and unfulfilling.

✷ ARCANA 19 ✷

You encounter relationship difficulties when pride, control and superiority dominate your actions. Behaviours like clinging to the past, being overly sensitive and seeking validation push partners away. Self-criticism and extremes in behaviour hinder emotional balance, while stress reactions and fault-finding create tension. Issues such as egocentrism and insecurity block intimacy, while attention-seeking makes connections feel superficial. Rejecting leadership and avoiding responsibility lead to imbalances; traits like narcissism and empty promises erode trust. Avoidance heightens challenges. Self-awareness, emotional balance and mutual respect are necessary to overcome these ego-driven behaviours.

✷ ARCANA 20 ✷

Your relationships can suffer when fear or resistance regarding family dynamics prevails. Avoiding connections with a partner's family or dismissing their perspectives may lead to separation. Issues such as excessive control, overprotection, dependency and fear of loss can also block harmony. Conflicts may stem from judgement or dissatisfaction with relatives, fixation on problems and lack of respect for family traditions. Then, negative patterns and rigid thinking further entrap you in destructive cycles. Balanced and fulfilling relationships will only come into being through respect, flexibility and the acceptance of family dynamics.

✷ ARCANA 21 ✷

You may encounter relationship challenges when emotional distance, withdrawal and dissatisfaction prevail. Extreme dependence, excessive independence or desiring immediate gratification can all make partners feel disconnected, while unrealistic standards of financial status, appearance or personal development will lead to a quick loss of interest. Narrow search areas, rigid boundaries and difficulty letting partners open up will further hinder intimacy. Withdrawal, fear of communication, social isolation, phobias or controlling tendencies will all create distance. Constant dissatisfaction and unaddressed fears can also destabilize relationships, rendering them stressful and unfulfilling.

✷ ARCANA 22 ✷

You may struggle in relationships if you fear losing your freedom or lead a dissolute lifestyle. Obsessive control, irresponsibility and emotional extremes can push your partner away, while unhealed childhood wounds, inner child trauma or a habit of hiding behind seriousness will prevent genuine connection. Conflicts can arise from neglecting responsibilities and engaging in chaotic or reckless behaviour. Infidelity and addictions will further hinder closeness. Genuine connection will only be possible if you take responsibility, seek emotional balance and avoid controlling or extreme reactions.

YOUR IDEAL PARTNER

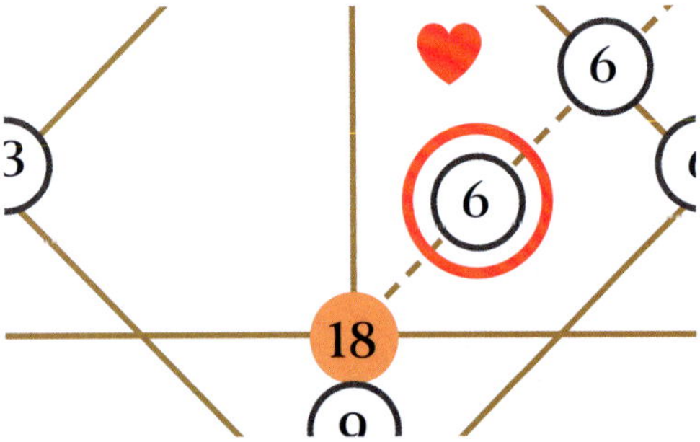

Your Ideal Partner

✷ ARCANA 3 ✷

You are likely to encounter your ideal partner in settings related to beauty, comfort and creativity, such as musical or crafting groups. They will emerge during a time of significant life pursuits, like building a business or home. They are emotionally attentive, generous and value quality, creating a secure environment for you. They may have financial stability or be working towards it and possesses family-oriented values. The relationship brings shared goals and a balance of roles, with you inspiring and nurturing while they support and provide.

✷ ARCANA 4 ✷

You are likely to find your ideal partner in business, government and leadership settings. They will emerge when you are grounded in your life and not trying to control everything. They are strong, reliable, self-sufficient, financially secure and value stability and responsibility. The relationship is marked by equality, respect and balance, where neither partner depends emotionally or financially on the other, but supports their growth while embodying their respective roles of Empress and Emperor.

✷ ARCANA 5 ✷

You will be likely to find your ideal partner in structured environments such as educational or legal institutions. They are characterized by reliability, maturity and a respect for tradition and family ties. They appreciate calm communication and philosophical discussions, often serving as a mentor, while you embody the role of teacher and moral guide, so you complement each other's strengths and shared values.

✷ ARCANA 6 ✷

Your ideal partner is likely to be found in environments that promote beauty, warmth and emotional connection, like celebrations and online communities. Often, love develops from pre-existing friendships or partnerships rather than spontaneous encounters. Your partner is characterized by gentleness, romanticism, emotional openness, attention to aesthetics and the ability to create a harmonious atmosphere. They are sociable, tactful and prioritize warmth and sincere communication. A successful relationship will involve you committing to them intentionally and wholeheartedly, rather than chasing illusions.

✷ ARCANA 7 ✷

You are likely to find your ideal partner in dynamic environments characterized by movement, ambition and leadership, such as business settings, military structures, sports spaces and education-focused platforms. They will emerge during a period of personal growth, when you are actively pursuing clear goals. They are characterized by strength, energy and leadership qualities, possessing a clear direction in life and an inclination towards continual development and new challenges. Their inspiring drive, individuality and confidence enable them to stand out and bring a sense of purpose to collaborative endeavours with you.

✷ ARCANA 8 ✷

You are likely to meet your ideal partner in environments that emphasize calmness, structure and responsibility, such as business, legal, media and self-development spaces. They are mature, grounded and socially established, often holding a respected role and having strong connections. They will emerge when you are living authentically, embodying integrity and pursuing balance rather than control. Professionally strict and confident, they adopt a softer approach in private. They value fairness, order and reliability, enabling you to make thoughtful decisions collaboratively.

✷ ARCANA 9 ✷

You are likely to find your ideal partner in serene and contemplative settings that prioritize depth, knowledge and personal growth, such as intellectual or scientific arenas, spiritual retreats, journeys and nature walks. The connection typically develops organically and gradually through reflective conversations and a lack of pressure. Your partner embodies wisdom, calmness and self-sufficiency, and has a preference for a tranquil, private life over constant social engagement. Often linked to fields such as science, medicine, psychology or healing, they are also dependable, patient, disciplined and detail-oriented.

✷ ARCANA 10 ✷

You are likely to meet your ideal partner in lively, creative and social environments where communication, teamwork, travel and new experiences are happening at events and parties or on business trips or online communities. They are easy-going, adventurous and sociable, full of energy and spontaneity, yet practical and responsible. They inspire you, bring joy and luck into your life, love movement and new experiences, and share your sense of humour. With them, you feel motivated, free and supported, and together you navigate life with ease, spontaneity and a sense of adventure.

✷ ARCANA 11 ✷

You are likely to meet your ideal partner in environments full of activity, energy and movement, such as sports, tourism or show business venues and areas focused on self-knowledge or spiritual growth. They are active, resilient and have a cheerful, open disposition with an unconventional sense of humour. They are strong both physically and mentally, full of energy, emotionally and sexually vibrant, and able to take responsibility and lead in the relationship. You inspire each other, channel your strengths into creative and constructive projects, and unlock each other's potential.

✷ ARCANA 12 ✷

You are likely to meet your ideal partner in creative and artistic environments, in helping professions, education, volunteer or charity projects or self-discovery and spiritual events. You may also encounter them in everyday settings where people are brought together involuntarily, like elevators, queues, hospital wards or traffic jams. They are innovative, creative, intuitive, gentle and compassionate. They think unconventionally, are emotionally mature and self-sufficient, and are ready to support and understand you. They are romantic, attentive and caring, valuing emotional security and a soulful, sincere connection, which allows both of you to grow while respecting each other's freedom and individuality.

✷ ARCANA 13 ✷

You are likely to find your ideal partner through adventurous, high-energy or transformative activities: sports, travel, relocations, rescue work, business projects or personal growth trainings. They are daring, unpredictable and fearless, full of curiosity and creativity, and emotionally and physically resilient. They sweep you off your feet with their charisma and vibrant energy, often initiating exciting changes in your life. Decisive and persistent, they thrive on passion, growth and new experiences with you. Together, you embrace constant change and adventure and enjoy a dynamic and invigorating relationship.

✷ ARCANA 14 ✷

You are likely to meet your ideal partner in spaces that nourish the soul, creativity and emotional growth: art galleries, exhibitions, conferences, cultural and historical sites, healing centres, spiritual growth events and during travels or tours, particularly in nature. They are sensitive, emotionally balanced and insightful, with a rich inner world. Gentle, compassionate, easy to communicate with and able to listen deeply, they create a calm, supportive and safe atmosphere for you. They appreciate beauty, nature and tenderness, and in the relationship, they share warmth, emotional intimacy and heartfelt connection, encouraging mutual care, understanding and the exploration of your inner worlds.

✷ ARCANA 15 ✷

You are likely to encounter your ideal partner in environments connected to helping, business, luxury, self-development, and high-level social or professional activity, such as self-discovery workshops, coaching sessions and luxury or entertainment venues. They are energetic, adventurous and sociable, and love life, abundance and exciting experiences. Passionate, generous and confident, with a strong sense of personal power, yet balanced and disciplined, they inspire you, motivate growth and share sensuality, passion and emotional intensity. Together, you thrive on adventure, prosperity and spiritual and emotional development, learning to manage impulses, passions and power responsibly.

✷ ARCANA 16 ✷

You are likely to meet your ideal partner in places where change, growth and hands-on activity happen, such as construction sites, training sessions, seminars, conferences and fitness and sports venues. They are someone who sees paths for improvement in everyday life and enjoys helping reconstruct or transform the world around them. Creative, innovative, responsible and disciplined but also unpredictable and lively, they bring excitement, drama or adventure into your life. They can be a spiritual mentor or teacher for you, guiding both of you towards growth, while supporting your shared spiritual and practical transformation.

✷ ARCANA 17 ✷

You are likely to find your ideal partner in creative, artistic or beauty-focused environments, such as cultural events, galleries, creative workshops and beauty salons, as well as in the helping professions and on retreats and self-discovery courses. They are bright, creative, stylish, sensitive and sociable, with a rich imagination and often 'star quality'. They inspire you and open your eyes to art and beauty, and you thrive when you support each other's creative paths, spend time in nature, travel and share spiritual or artistic experiences.

✷ ARCANA 18 ✷

You are likely to meet your ideal partner in creative and artistic fields, show business, beauty and helping professions, near bodies of water, on journeys or night walks, or in places connected to philosophy, art and traditions, especially around the full moon. They are spiritually aware, imaginative and positive-minded. Mysterious and enigmatic, with a rich inner world, they value safety, intimacy and private time together. While they may seem closed off, even secretive, in public, in one-on-one moments they are sweet, sensitive and vulnerable. Responsible, transparent and grounded, using their imagination to create rather than distort reality, they will help you overcome your fears and support you in life.

✷ ARCANA 19 ✷

You are likely to meet your ideal partner in public and social spaces, at events aimed at the general population, or on beaches and in sunny outdoor locations. They are bright, open and radiate positive energy. Lively, spontaneous and emotionally uninhibited, with a sense of childlike joy and artistic flair, they stand out in a crowd through their appearance or unconventional manners and are capable of leadership. Confident and financially secure, they enjoy life and are generous with love, attention and surprises. They bring joy, love and excitement into your life, while encouraging you to shine and express yourself fully.

✷ ARCANA 20 ✷

You are likely to meet your ideal partner in fields connected to information, business, helping, the family, the media, science, government and spiritual practices. Introductions may also come through relatives or people from other nations. Your partner is responsible, caring and family-oriented, valuing children and time spent together as a family. They are also intuitive, mystical and unpredictable, with a clear worldview and beliefs that align with yours. While they may appear distant or reserved in public, in private they show empathy, support and understanding. They will respect your freedom of choice and action while helping you resolve ancestral patterns, family issues and karmic tasks.

✷ ARCANA 21 ✷

You are likely to meet your ideal partner in international or cross-cultural settings, in business, public service, large-scale projects, the helping professions, the internet, the media, charity ventures, spiritual practices, when travelling, or in any other sphere that involves expanding consciousness and engaging globally. They are curious, perceptive and peace-loving, with a global mindset and a broad, erudite perspective. They love to travel and thrive on exploring the world and different cultures and ideas. Original, unpredictable and intellectually stimulating, they have a complex inner world and a talent for captivating storytelling. They will bring abundance, opportunities and freedom to your partnership, and together, you will expand your horizons, explore the world and live without limitations.

✷ ARCANA 22 ✷

You are likely to encounter your ideal partner in creative and artistic fields, the entertainment industry, the social or helping professions, progressive and scientific spheres, at events celebrating freedom or to do with international relations, on retreats or while doing spiritual practices or travelling. They are cheerful, easy-going, freedom-loving and adventurous. Spontaneous and playful, they know how to create joy and celebration in everyday life. Optimistic, sociable and artistic, they are able to let go of the past and embrace new experiences. They love intellectual and creative exploration, alongside fun and lighthearted pastimes. In the relationship, they value freedom for themselves and you, avoid unnecessary restriction, and bring positivity, adventure and humour into your shared life.

CHAPTER 9

YOUR PATH TO PROSPERITY

YOUR MONEY CHANNEL

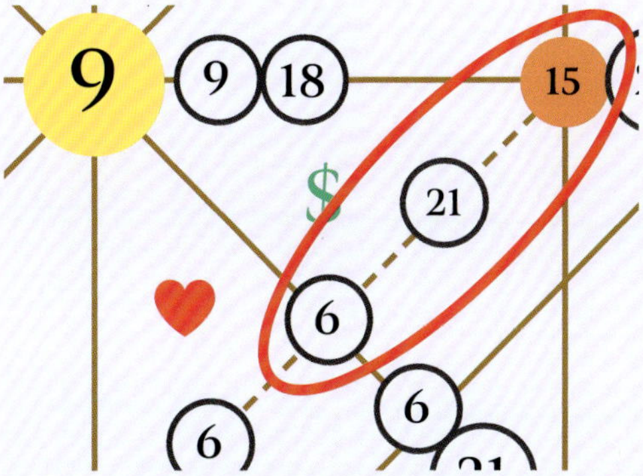

Your Money Channel

Your money channel in the Destiny Matrix provides insight into the factors that contribute to your financial well-being. It reveals the specific state of mind, behaviours and actions that are necessary for you to activate its energy.

The number shown in orange represents your path to finance. The number next to the dollar sign indicates your ideal career. In this figure, Arcana 21 appears in that position and the adjacent number, Arcana 6, describes how to balance your career and your relationship.

YOUR PROSPERITY BLOCKS

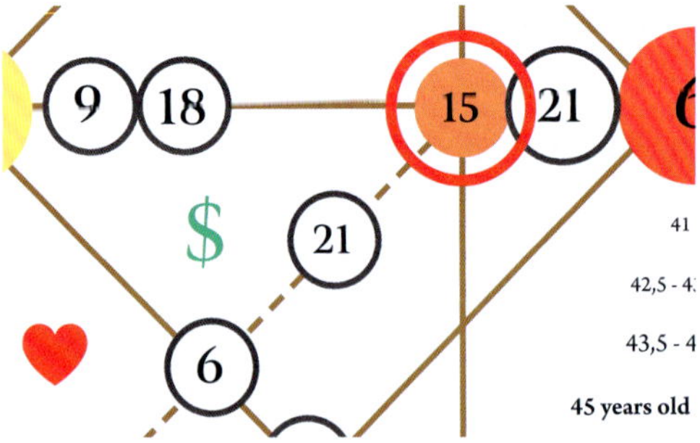

Your Prosperity Blocks

⁕ ARCANA 3 ⁕

Neglecting health and self-care, as well as avoiding responsibility and leadership, may be blocking your financial flow. Factors such as hyper-control and living beyond your means may also hinder money attraction. Forming strong, harmonious and collaborative relationships with peers and nurturing creative projects will attract wealth. Money comes through creative work, implementing projects, maintaining beauty and comfort, family continuity, caring for others and cultivating a sense of ownership and mastery over resources.

⁕ ARCANA 4 ⁕

For you, money flows may be hindered by the avoidance of leadership and responsibility, as well as poor interpersonal relationships and negative emotions. Poor relationships and competition with men, distrust, resentment towards a father figure, eternal dissatisfaction, impatience and a lack of gratitude further block abundance. Positive financial outcomes are associated with wise leadership, effective resource management, cooperation, healing relationships with male figures (especially fathers or male mentors) and gratitude. Engage in new ventures, control resources effectively, run your own business, handle negotiations and offer charity or provide jobs for others to improve your financial flow.

✷ ARCANA 5 ✷

Rigid thinking and a narrow view of income may hinder your financial flow. Stagnation occurs when you stop learning or cling to outdated methods. Resistance to change, fear of competition and unresolved family conflicts also block money flow. However, financial opportunities increase with flexibility, continuous learning and nurturing relationships. Income may come through teaching and sharing knowledge, while adhering to legal responsibilities also enhances financial health. Lead by example and give knowledge freely to foster a responsive financial environment.

✷ ARCANA 6 ✷

You may hinder your financial flow by settling for less, hoarding savings, pursuing discounts or doubting your worth. Financial blocks may also arise from perfectionism, indecision, imitating others and ignoring your uniqueness. On the other hand, money flows when you value yourself, embrace joy and beauty, engage in meaningful connections and invest in your passions. Cultivate harmony and share warmth with others to foster abundance and allow wealth to manifest by expressing love freely and authentically.

✷ ARCANA 7 ✷

Living in a state of aggression and haste may block your financial flow by causing burnout and chaotic actions. Income slows when you work in isolation, compete aggressively or become passive. Conversely, financial success arises from having clear goals and collaborating with others through teamwork and shared aspirations. Plan strategically, maintain an active lifestyle and build mutually beneficial partnerships to improve your financial flow.

✷ ARCANA 8 ✷

Your financial flow may be hindered by resentment, the aggressive pursuit of justice and negative emotions. Blockages arise from refusing to admit mistakes and holding grudges and negative beliefs about money. A lack of balance between giving and receiving leads to negative money energy. Conversely, financial prosperity is achieved through honesty, responsibility and a clear structure. Release resentment, maintain fairness and act in alignment with your positive values to restore balance and make money that lasts.

✷ ARCANA 9 ✷

For you, financial flow may be hindered by intellectual or spiritual pride, negative views of others, emotional isolation or rejection of the material world. Excessive saving, neglecting personal well-being and living with less may also block income. Conversely, financial abundance comes when you respect the balance between spiritual and material needs, have self-worth, invest in well-being and share knowledge with others. Engage in teaching, mentoring or consulting, focus on self-care and be open with others to enhance your finances.

✷ ARCANA 10 ✷

To enable finance to flow, it's essential for you to establish clear goals and actively pursue them rather than passively relying on luck or external expectations. Money flow may be obstructed by fear, tension and joyless labour. Finances will improve when you align with your natural flow, take consistent actions and maintain a relaxed attitude, allowing opportunities to emerge through your connections. Embrace teamwork, gratitude, freelancing and open communication to foster abundance and allow money to circulate freely.

✷ ARCANA 11 ✷

You may be restricting your financial flow by living in constant stress about money, whether as a result of hoarding it or spending it impulsively. Financial setbacks occur when you rush, scatter your energy or plunge into workaholism without rest. Moreover, ignoring your health or oscillating between extreme effort and exhaustion will block the flow. Money will come to you through conscious energy management, maintaining physical vitality and inspiring others. Pace yourself, plan wisely and allow for pleasure and rest to expand your financial potential.

✷ ARCANA 12 ✷

Your financial flow may be hindered by a victim mentality, along with complaining, over-giving and sacrificing yourself while seeking appreciation. Fear of charging, difficulty in setting prices and allowing others to exploit your time and energy also contribute to financial loss. Stagnation occurs when you suppress your voice, manipulate situations or cling to old habits due to guilt. Money flows when you acknowledge your self-worth, set clear boundaries and establish fair exchanges for work. Learn to give without self-sacrifice, to accept help and engage in compassionate, creative and honest service while prioritizing self-care and saying 'no' when necessary.

✷ ARCANA 13 ✷

You hinder your financial flow through stagnation, fear of change, disorganization and unfinished projects. Money is lost when you cling to the past, resist development, neglect your finances or take unjustified risks. Cluttered thoughts, spaces and outdated attitudes also hinder abundance. Conversely, embracing change, starting new projects and regularly transforming your approach will enhance it. Innovation, learning, travel and entrepreneurship also facilitate financial flow. Complete tasks and adapt to new opportunities while trusting your instincts to promote financial growth.

✷ ARCANA 14 ✷

You may find money flow obstructed by self-doubt, lack of creative expression and unfulfilling jobs. Factors like impulsivity, extreme habits and a lack of balance may also impede the flow, as may infantilism and the devaluation of desires. Conversely, financial well-being is achieved by following your soul, engaging in joyful work, expressing your talents, practising moderation and maintaining harmony in various aspects of life. Creative endeavours, artistic expression and mindful progress will naturally attract abundance.

✷ ARCANA 15 ✷

You may block your financial flow due to impulsivity, greed, selfishness and vanity. Chasing prestige or brands, giving in to hedonism or over-consumption, or failing to recognize your true desires can bring losses. Self-awareness, moderation and managing your desires are key to attracting wealth. Helping others and maintaining personal growth will also enhance financial flow. Calm spending and long-term engagement will contribute to stable finances, while rituals and a positive attitude will further attract prosperity.

✷ ARCANA 16 ✷

For you, money flow may be hindered by resistance to change, stagnation and unresolved emotions. Chaos, disorganization and a lack of planning may also block abundance. Personal development, adaptability and breaking old patterns will allow it to flow. Key factors include thoughtful planning, prioritization, organization and proactive behaviour. Endeavour to stay spiritually and physically strong, manage your energy and respond calmly and confidently to life's challenges to better your financial flow.

✷ ARCANA 17 ✷

You may hinder your financial flow through pride, negative self-perceptions and undervaluing others. Spending excessively for attention, engaging in unfulfilling work and isolating yourself may also obstruct monetary gain. Conversely, expressing your creativity and originality will attract abundance, and sharing skills and inspiring others will foster recognition and financial rewards. Networking, collaboration and social engagement are essential for opening financial opportunities. Trust in your abilities, express yourself and turn your creativity into something accessible and valuable to others.

✷ ARCANA 18 ✷

You may find money flow is impeded by negative emotions like fear, anxiety, resentment and envy. Additionally, poor investments, neglecting your intuition and a tendency to avoid responsibility can hinder wealth accumulation. Embracing positive thinking, disciplined focus and creative expression are key to fostering financial abundance. Utilizing your imagination through art, design, photography, handicrafts or innovative projects can lead to financial success, as can working in esoteric fields. Maintain a cosy, well-organized home and work environment, understand subconscious cues in yourself and others, and apply foresight to improve your money flow.

✷ ARCANA 19 ✷

Your money flow may be blocked by impulsive spending, selfishness, pride, authoritarianism, vanity and an excessive desire to be in the spotlight. Negative thinking, guilt, self-blame, resentment, indignation and fear of responsibility may be additional factors. Avoiding large projects, being unwilling to take social or organizational responsibility and failing to share your energy, light and opportunities with others will further limit your prosperity. It will flow, however, if you call on your strengths, radiate positivity and joy, and engage in leadership, public work and helping others succeed. Creativity, passion-driven work and charitable contributions also enhance your wealth attraction.

✷ ARCANA 20 ✷

You may be hindering your money flow through rejecting your family lineage and parental support, while taking on negative inherited attitudes. Selfishness, materialism and superficiality may also be obstructing your financial growth. Limiting beliefs may prevent access to opportunities. Conversely, embracing family roots, forgiving parents and addressing inherited money patterns can open financial flow. Strengthening family ties and supporting relatives will enhance your prosperity, while work benefiting your family or community will improve your money flow.

✷ ARCANA 21 ✷

Impatience and dissatisfaction may be leading to a closed mindset that hinders your financial growth. Negative attitudes such as aggression and intolerance, along with fears related to parental patterns and the avoidance of technology, will obstruct your financial opportunities. Conversely, you attract abundance by engaging in large-scale global projects, setting ambitious goals, utilizing technology and fostering cultural understanding. Be grateful for what you have, live within your means, do step-by-step planning, practise realistic financial management and build skills to adapt to different environments and cultures to strengthen your money flow.

✷ ARCANA 22 ✷

You may be obstructing your money flow through psychological factors like tension, obsession and extremes in spending, as well as fear of change and rigid routines. Naivety, irresponsibility, fear of leaving a familiar but uninspiring job, attachment to people, place or routine, and a rigid schedule or unhealthy lifestyle may also be contributing. Conversely, money flows freely when approached with creativity, pleasure and flexibility. Engaging in activities that promote enjoyment, independence and liberation, such as travel and creative projects, will activate your financial energy. Enjoy life and express your inner child to strengthen your financial flow.

YOUR IDEAL CAREER

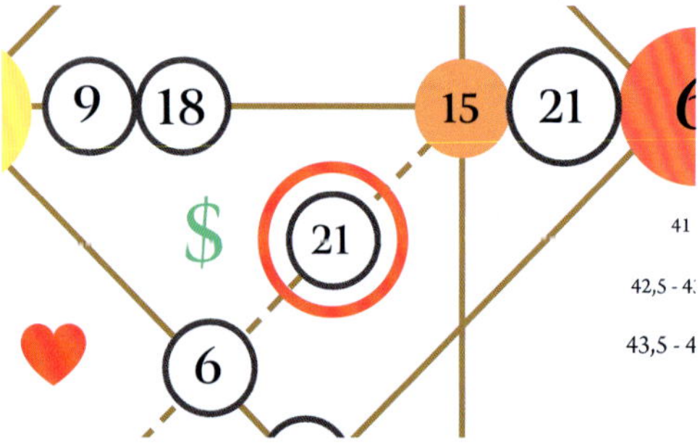

Your Ideal Career

✷ ARCANA 3 ✷

Actor, administrator, animator, caregiver, choreographer, confectioner, cook, cosmetologist, dancer, director, educator, entrepreneur, event organizer, farmer, fashion designer, fitness trainer, gardener, gynaecologist, hairdresser, image maker, interior designer, make-up artist, manager, manicurist, methodologist, model, nanny, nurse, paediatrician, psychologist, psychotherapist, recruitment manager, stylist, teacher, TV presenter.

✷ ARCANA 4 ✷

Actor, administrator, architect, auto mechanic, banker, bricklayer, builder, business owner, carpenter, cosmetologist, director, electrician, entrepreneur, estate agent, event organizer, factory worker, farmer, foreman, government official, hairdresser, image maker, interior designer, investigator, lawyer, lecturer, manager, manicurist, marketer, mayor, mechanic, mediator, military professional, minister, nanny, negotiator, painter, personnel manager, plasterer, police officer, politician, psychologist, public relations specialist, stylist, teacher, technician, technologist, tractor driver, welder.

✷ ARCANA 5 ✷

Accountant, analyst, auditor, bailiff, bank teller, banker, biologist, bookbinder, cashier, chemist, commercial director, consultant, course creator, credit consultant, economist, engineer, entrepreneur, estate agent, financier, government employee, historian, inspector, insurance agent, judge, lawyer, lecturer, legislator, linguist, machinist, manager, mechanic, minister, programmer, psychologist, publisher, religious scholar, scientist, securities market specialist, spiritual teacher, surveyor, teacher, technician.

✷ ARCANA 6 ✷

Administrator, animator, artist, call centre operator, content manager, copywriter, cosmetologist, costume designer, dancer, decorator, designer, director, DJ, exhibition organizer, fashion designer, florist, hairdresser, human resources manager, image maker, jeweller, journalist, lighting designer, make-up artist, marketer, mediator, model, musician, organizer, performer, photographer, producer, psychologist, publisher, sales manager, screenwriter, set designer, sound engineer, stylist, television journalist, trainer, translator, TV presenter, visual content creator, writer.

✷ ARCANA 7 ✷

Athlete, bailiff, banker, bodybuilder, bodyguard, choreographer, coach, conductor, customs officer, dancer, executive, fitness instructor, flight attendant, footballer, forensic expert, government official, industrial climber, investigator, IT specialist, jockey, judge, lawyer, logistics manager, manager, mechanic, mentor, military professional, minister, motivator, notary, operational officer, pilot, police officer, prosecutor, racer, rescuer, sailor, scout, ship's captain, sports instructor, stunt performer, swimmer, taxi driver, team leader, trainer, transport specialist, travel professional, truck driver, wrestler.

✷ ARCANA 8 ✷

Accountant, analyst, art therapist, business owner, cashier, department head, document manager, economist, editor, entrepreneur, executive, finance professional, healer, historian, human rights activist, journalist, law enforcement officer, lawyer, manager, mathematician, military professional, political commentator, politician, psychoanalyst, psychologist, public figure, secretary, social worker, systems analyst, tax official, trader.

✷ ARCANA 9 ✷

Accountant, anthropologist, archaeologist, archivist, astrologer, author, banker, biologist, blogger, chemist, copywriter, cultural researcher, designer, doctor, draftsperson, economist, editor, engineer, ethnographer, financial analyst, forester, geographer, historian, IT professional, journalist, librarian, linguist, marketer, mathematician, methodologist, pharmacist, philosopher, physicist, priest, programmer, psychologist, researcher, scientist, screenwriter, SEO specialist, spiritual practitioner, surveyor, teacher, technologist, theologian, translator, writer.

✷ ARCANA 10 ✷

Administrator, art director, assistant, astrologer, bartender, brand manager, business owner, casino worker, coach, conductor, consultant, creative designer, developer, driver, entrepreneur, event organizer, foreman, freelancer, HR specialist, journalist, logistics specialist, marketer, merchandiser, motivator, numerologist, organizer, performer, presenter, programmer, psychologist, public relations specialist, recruiter, salesperson, sports professional, team leader, trainer, translator, travel professional, waiter.

✷ ARCANA 11 ✷

Advertiser, bodyguard, builder, coach, construction worker, customs officer, energy healer, firefighter, fitness trainer, journalist, leader, manager, marketer, masseur, military professional, miner, official, painter, police officer, politician, promoter, public relations specialist, racer, repair worker, rescuer, sailor, social media marketer, trainer, welder.

✷ ARCANA 12 ✷

Actor, artist, biologist, charity worker, chemist, designer, director, educator, fashion designer, geneticist, hair stylist, healer, inventor, medical professional, methodologist, musician, personal branding specialist, project engineer, psychologist, public relations specialist, radio technician, scientist, screenwriter, social worker, tattoo artist, teacher, technologist, veterinarian, writer, zoologist.

✷ ARCANA 13 ✷

Actor, advertiser, blogger, chiropractor, coach, emergency responder, esoteric practitioner, forensic expert, geneticist, healer, intelligence officer, investigator, marketer, massage therapist, medical professional, military professional, pathologist, pilot, police officer, psychologist, public relations specialist, racer, reporter, rescuer, sailor, security professional, stunt performer, surgeon, traveller, virologist.

✷ ARCANA 14 ✷

Actor, architect, art historian, artist, biologist, camera operator, chemist, composer, confectioner, costume designer, dancer, designer, director, DJ, doctor, environmental worker, exhibition organizer, fashion model, florist, hairdresser, healer, herbalist, historian, icon painter, image maker, jeweller, journalist, laboratory specialist, livestock breeder, make-up artist, masseur, medical professional, musician, pharmacist, photographer, playwright, priest, producer, psychologist, screenwriter, sculptor, show business professional, singer, sound engineer, tourism professional, veterinarian, writer, zoologist.

✷ ARCANA 15 ✷

Actor, addiction counsellor, advertiser, ambassador, analyst, artist, banker, broker, business owner, casino operation manager, coach, comedian, consultant, crisis manager, diagnostic specialist, director, entrepreneur, esoteric practitioner, estate agent, financier, government official, healer, investigator, journalist, judge, lawyer, manager, mentor, minister, modelling professional, musician, performer, pilot, producer, psychologist, reporter, scriptwriter, security professional, senior manager, spiritual practitioner, trader.

✷ ARCANA 16 ✷

Acrobat, archaeologist, architect, auto mechanic, builder, coach, construction worker, content manager, crisis manager, designer, director, electrician, engineer, geologist, gunsmith, healer, investigator, IT professional, manager, massage therapist, medical professional, miner, oil worker, photographer, psychologist, public relations specialist, repair technician, spiritual trainer, teacher, trainer, utilities worker.

✷ ARCANA 17 ✷

Actor, advertiser, animator, artist, astrologer, astronomer, beauty professional, blogger, bioenergy therapist, camera operator, conductor, cosmonaut, creator, decorator, designer, director, DJ, editor, event host, exhibition organizer, florist, healer, herbalist, illustrator, image maker, journalist, jeweller, landscape designer, make up artist, medical professional, meteorologist, musician, organizer, performer, photographer, poet, polar researcher, psychic, public relations specialist, screenwriter, singer, spiritual trainer, stylist, teacher, television and radio presenter, tourism professional, trade professional, veterinarian, writer.

✷ ARCANA 18 ✷

Actor, architect, artist, bioenergy therapist, camera operator, choreographer, cosmetologist, creator, depth psychologist, designer, detective, director, engineer, exposure specialist, fashion designer, fashion worker, film director, fortune-teller, game developer, hairdresser, healing specialist, illusionist, illustrator, intelligence officer, journalist, linguist, magician, make-up artist, medical professional, natural healer, photographer, producer, psychologist, self-knowledge specialist, stylist, system developer, television worker, writer.

✷ ARCANA 19 ✷

Actor, administrator, artist, business owner, designer, diplomat, electrician, event organizer, festival organizer, firefighter, head of children's home, leader, manager, military enterprise manager, musician, network marketer, orator, philanthropist, producer, public figure, researcher, sales manager, salesperson, scientist, singer, social worker, spiritual teacher, teacher.

✷ ARCANA 20 ✷

Actor, administrator, advertiser, archaeologist, artist, banker, business owner, content manager, copywriter, dentist, designer, dispatcher, economist, engineer, entrepreneur, family psychologist, forensic expert, freelancer, game developer, healer, historian, IT specialist, journalist, judge, lawyer, methodologist, musician, obstetrician, pathologist, photographer, programmer, psychologist, publisher, radio operator, researcher, security professional, singer, system administrator, teacher, translator, webmaster, writer.

✷ ARCANA 21 ✷

Activist, actor, artist, aviation worker, banker, bioenergy therapist, charity worker, dancer, diplomat, director, driver, economist, ethnographer, exhibition organizer, financier, flight attendant, guide, healer, historian, information specialist, investor, journalist, leader, linguist, missionary, musician, orator, organizer, philanthropist, pilot, politician, programmer, show business professional, social worker, translator, travel professional, writer.

✷ ARCANA 22 ✷

Actor, artist, circus performer, computer specialist, diplomat, driver, entertainer, explorer, freelance artist, geologist, journalist, leader, mountaineer, parachutist, performer, pilot, poet, political activist, programmer, psychologist, researcher, rock-climber, self-development trainer, show host, spiritual healer, tourism professional, traveller, writer.

BALANCING LOVE AND FINANCE

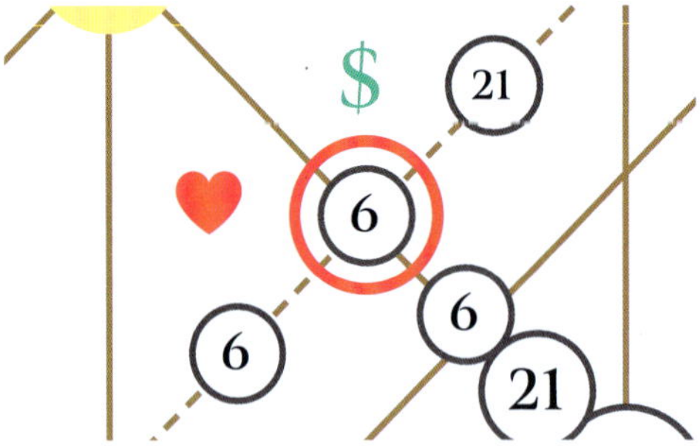

Balancing Love And Finance

✷ ARCANA 3 ✷

You balance love and finance by communicating your feelings calmly and honestly, creating a peaceful home and treating your relationship as a shared project in which care, responsibility and beauty matter. You invest time and money in consciously improving your space, planning experiences together and supporting each other without losing your own independence or self-worth. When you value yourself, respect boundaries with your family, nurture romance and approach money as a tool for comfort and growth rather than for control, you create a partnership with both emotional security and financial stability.

✷ ARCANA 4 ✷

You balance love and finance by speaking openly about your needs with honesty and warmth, planning spending together without pressure or blame and treating financial decisions as a shared responsibility rather than a power struggle. You communicate using your feelings instead of accusations, practise gratitude and appreciation daily, and make space for rest, romance and personal growth alongside budgeting and goal-setting. When you respect each other's limits, invest jointly in both emotional closeness and financial awareness, and give as much care as you receive, love and money stop competing and start supporting each other.

✷ ARCANA 5 ✷

You balance love and finance by making your partnership clear, structured and intentional, treating both emotional and material matters with responsibility and respect. You align on shared goals early, formalize commitments, create family traditions and keep your home and money organized together. When you have self-control instead of control over others, listen deeply, learn from each other and approach challenges as lessons rather than conflicts, your relationship becomes stable, trusting and financially grounded at the same time.

✷ ARCANA 6 ✷

You balance love and finance by leading with unconditional love, generosity and self-worth, while staying emotionally independent and grounded in yourself. You give care, attention and gifts without expectations, nurture romance and joy in everyday life, and heal your inner child so you don't seek money or love to fill emotional gaps. When you love openly, value yourself and share from abundance rather than need, emotional fulfilment naturally supports material stability, and money flows as a reflection of inner harmony rather than a substitute for love.

✷ ARCANA 7 ✷

You balance love and finance by moving forwards as a team, setting financial and other goals together while staying emotionally conscious and self-regulated. You track finances jointly, travel and stay active together to avoid stagnation, and treat success as mutual rather than competitive. Communicate through your own feelings, transform conflict and aggression into growth, and celebrate each other's wins to create a relationship where emotional connection fuels financial progress, and steady movement keeps both love and money flowing.

✷ ARCANA 8 ✷

You balance love and finance by consciously maintaining balance in all areas of life, not allowing work, money or emotions to overpower your relationship. You plan finances together, keep promises, respect boundaries and balance giving with receiving, work with rest, and logic with compassion. When you have self-control instead of control over others, listen deeply, forgive and regularly check in on your shared life balance, both emotional harmony and financial stability grow naturally and sustainably.

✷ ARCANA 9 ✷

You balance love and finance by staying deeply connected to your feelings, your body and your partner, instead of living only in your head or in survival mode. You listen to yourself, express your emotions honestly, respect personal space and don't neglect your own needs or desires, which prevents emotional emptiness from turning into financial anxiety or overspending. When you stay grounded, present and emotionally aware, you make calmer financial decisions and build a relationship where emotional security and material stability grow together.

✷ ARCANA 10 ✷

You balance love and finance by trusting your inner flow and making space for joy, intuition and shared meaning instead of forcing everything through logic or pressure. You listen to your feelings, move with your partner when life calls for rest or action, and allow flexibility in spending without guilt. When you stay playful, grateful, open to signs and emotionally aligned, financial decisions become lighter and clearer, and love grows naturally as both of you feel supported rather than controlled.

✷ ARCANA 11 ✷

You balance love and finance by consciously releasing excess energy through healthy activities like exercise, sports and shared recreation, keeping both your body and mind active. You plan finances together, set shared goals, create budgets and track progress equally, while also prioritizing rest, relaxation and quality time with your partner. With physical vitality, intellectual engagement and emotional care through communication, praise and shared leisure, your relationship will stay passionate, harmonious and financially grounded.

✷ ARCANA 12 ✷

You balance love and finance by setting clear boundaries, saying 'no' when needed and offering help only when it's truly wanted, which prevents resentment arising and preserves your energy. You cultivate creativity together, sharing art, music or other projects that strengthen your bond and open new opportunities. Accept compliments and generosity gracefully, give freely without expectations, and take responsibility for your life and choices. If you incorporate personal responsibility, mutual respect and creative energy into daily life, your partnership will thrive emotionally while your financial and personal resources will grow harmoniously.

✷ ARCANA 13 ✷

You balance love and finance by keeping your shared space and life energetically clear and organized. Regularly declutter, complete unfinished tasks and clean together, which will refresh both emotional and financial energy. Introduce new experiences, creative projects and reasonable challenges to keep your relationship dynamic and inspired. Periodic detoxes, whether of food, digital devices or mental clutter, renew your energy, while practices such as writing and releasing negative emotions prevent stagnation. Combine active care for your home, creativity and emotional processing to maintain a vibrant, loving partnership while freeing energy for financial growth and opportunity.

✷ ARCANA 14 ✷

You balance love and finance by bringing fluidity, calm and intention into both your relationship and your finances. Practices involving water – showers, baths, meditation by rivers or the sea, and even drinking water with affirmations – refresh your emotional and financial state. If you create rituals, enjoy spa or sauna sessions together and cultivate creativity through photography, art or journalling, you will both strengthen your bond and stimulate the flow of abundance. Introduce mindful ascetic practices and heartfelt affirmations to transform discipline into energy for growth, and enjoy shared leisure and spiritual exploration, which will aid both love and financial flow.

✷ ARCANA 15 ✷

You balance love and finance by cultivating awareness, passion and responsibility together. By exploring your desires, experimenting creatively and honouring pleasure in daily life, you strengthen trust, intimacy and mutual appreciation. At the same time, you engage your money energy consciously, learning financial literacy, playing money transformation games and making playful yet deliberate financial decisions. Combine sensuality, creativity and responsible handling of resources to ensure that your partnership thrives emotionally, physically and materially.

✷ ARCANA 16 ✷

You balance love and finance by treating your life and home as a dynamic, creative space. Regularly declutter, reorganize and refresh your surroundings to release stagnant energy and invite abundance in. Share detox practices, mindful routines and meditations to stay aligned emotionally and mentally. Approach challenges with gratitude and reflection, transforming conflicts into lessons. Use ascetic practices and intentional changes to direct energy into growth, purpose and financial well-being. Cultivate conscious creativity, thoughtful communication and deliberate action so that your relationship thrives both emotionally and materially.

✷ ARCANA 17 ✷

You balance love and finance by embracing your 'star energy', and by showing up fully in life and in your partnership. Attend events together, experiment with your looks and explore creative activities that inspire both joy and financial growth. Share photoshoots, workshops and masterclasses to expand creativity and confidence. Follow your intuition and impulses, using small exercises to guide decisions and desires. Support each other's talents, celebrating successes and visualizing shared goals so that your partnership and money energy shine in harmony, while blending self-expression with practical abundance.

✷ ARCANA 18 ✷

You balance love and finance by combining playful rituals, mindfulness and shared intentions with practical awareness. Use talismans, water practices, vision boards and lighthearted money superstitions to attract abundance, while keeping a positive mental focus and letting go of negativity. Spend quality time together reading, walking, meditating and enjoying intimate moments to strengthen your bond. Respect each other's inner worlds and face financial fears together with conscious exercises. Blend intention, creativity and shared experiences to make your relationship and financial energy grow in harmony.

✷ ARCANA 19 ✷

You balance love and finance by cultivating gratitude, shared energy and playful intention. Begin each day together with morning rituals, sun exposure and writing exercises to set a positive tone for both your partnership and financial energy. Use symbolic talismans, vision plates and cheerful, lighthearted rituals to focus on abundance while keeping the process fun and stress-free. Avoid controlling each other and share both creative and physical activities to release energy constructively. Combine gratitude, joy and mindful interaction to keep your love vibrant and your financial flow strong.

✷ ARCANA 20 ✷

You balance love and finance by understanding and honouring your family and ancestral influences, recognizing patterns around relationships and money and consciously choosing what to carry forwards. Together, explore your lineages, celebrate positive traits and release limiting beliefs about money or love. Creating family trees, sharing stories and performing gratitude and reconciliation rituals with your ancestors will strengthen your bond and provide a foundation for trust, abundance and mutual support. Acknowledge inherited patterns and actively cultivate harmony to align your relationship and financial energy, turning past lessons into present strengths.

✷ ARCANA 21 ✷

You balance love and finance by combining shared visions with grounded planning. Explore desires, dreams and goals together, whether for travel, learning or experiences, while staying mindful of the practical steps. Practise gratitude daily, celebrate small joys and support each other emotionally, nurturing both love and self-love and reducing blame or tension. Experiment, learn new skills and involve each other in decisions to create a dynamic, playful partnership where shared experiences and mutual encouragement aid both relationship and financial growth.

✷ ARCANA 22 ✷

You balance love and finance by blending gratitude, playfulness and mindful decision-making into your daily life. Keep a shared gratitude journal for both what you have and what you wish to receive, celebrate small wins and release attachments that no longer serve you. Make choices together by noticing your bodily responses and intuition and use tools like cards or playful exercises to clarify intentions. Cultivate joy and creativity by reconnecting with your inner children and engaging in games, spontaneous adventures and shared experiences. Honour each other's desires, nurture curiosity and approach life lightly to create a relationship where emotional richness and financial well-being support each other naturally.

CHAPTER 10

YOUR PURPOSE

YOUR PERSONAL PURPOSE (AGE 20–40)

Soul searching, balance of feminine and masculine qualities, abilities, skills.

Code:

Sky: b+d= (h)
Earth: a+c= (j)
h+j= (k)

Example:

Sky: 8+9= (17)
Earth: 22+6= (10*)
17+10= (9**)

** Sum totals cannot exceed 22; 28 reduced is 2+8=10*
*** Sum totals cannot exceed 22; 27 reduced is 2+7=9*

Your Personal Purpose

Here, you calculate your Sky number by adding the numbers located at the top and bottom of your sky line. You calculate your Earth number by adding the numbers positioned at both ends of the Earth line. By adding the resulting Sky and Earth numbers together, you obtain your personal purpose: the point where spiritual intention and material experience unite.

True fulfilment and a sense of wholeness arise when both the spiritual and material aspects of life are honoured and integrated. Ignoring either the spiritual or material side leads to restlessness and a feeling that something essential is missing.

✷ ARCANA 3 ✷

You are here to create growth, abundance and stability in the material world while staying spiritually generous and balanced. Money is a result, not your goal. Your task is to build something meaningful – family, traditions, projects or a legacy – and to share your knowledge, creativity and care with others. Create beauty, comfort and order, and use material things as tools, not attachments. You are meant to step fully into your natural role, nurturing, leading and protecting in a healthy way. Honour your connection with your parents, especially your mother, while becoming independent and mature.

✷ ARCANA 4 ✷

You are here to build a stable, abundant life by using your strength wisely and creating lasting foundations in family, work and personal projects. Take responsibility for your actions, maintain clear and honest relationships and honour your parents while becoming independent. Form partnerships based on equality, support your loved ones and guide children or others with care while teaching strength, responsibility and compassion. Avoid controlling others or micromanaging their lives; instead, lead with integrity, balance and fairness. Focus on practical growth, forgiveness, gratitude and letting go of stress so that you can achieve harmony, success and well-being without unnecessary conflict or tension.

✷ ARCANA 5 ✷

You are here to grow continuously through learning, self-development and deepening your knowledge. Stagnation weakens you; progress keeps you aligned. Your path involves education, research and spiritual or intellectual exploration, while building strong family ties and a broad worldview. You are meant to share wisdom clearly and calmly, without preaching or controlling others. Respect different perspectives, allow people their own choices and live your own life rather than fulfilling others' expectations.

✷ ARCANA 6 ✷

You are here to learn self-love and self-acceptance. Your task is not perfection, but growth: turning mistakes into experience and moving forwards with kindness towards yourself. Trust your worth, beauty and significance, knowing you exist for a reason. You are meant to live with an open heart, create loving and harmonious relationships and bring warmth, beauty and balance into the world. Build strong family bonds and inspire and support those close to you, while also nurturing your own passions.

✷ ARCANA 7 ✷

You are here to win through movement, action and forward momentum. Your strengths are leadership, drive and the ability to take control of your life. Set clear goals, manage your emotions and turn intensity into focused progress rather than pressure. You thrive when you stay active, explore new places and keep evolving. Lead not only for yourself, but for the good of your family, team and a greater purpose. Choose peaceful, conscious ways to succeed, balance action with inner calm and avoid burnout.

✷ ARCANA 8 ✷

You are here to observe, not judge. Your task is to see meaning and lessons in everything that happens, understanding cause and effect rather than blaming or condemning. Life is your teacher, and every challenge is an experience your soul chose for growth. You are meant to maintain inner balance, live consciously and take full responsibility for your life. Let go of resentment, aggression and the need to divide the world into right and wrong. Study the laws of life, karma and energy exchange, and apply them with humility.

✷ ARCANA 9 ✷

You are here to live in balance between spirit and matter, logic and intuition, solitude and connection. Your task is to enjoy earthly life while growing spiritually, honouring wisdom from your family, ancestors and ancient knowledge as you discover your own path. You are meant to trust yourself, share your knowledge and develop both intellect and intuition. Open your heart to people, release old resentments and build deep, honest relationships. Allow yourself prosperity without guilt, care for your health and respect your natural cycles of retreat and connection.

✷ ARCANA 10 ✷

You are here to live in trust, ease and flow. Your task is to relax, enjoy life and believe in your own luck. Move with life instead of controlling it, listen to your intuition and make choices based on what your soul truly wants. You are meant to stay active, social and open to opportunities, while living in the present with gratitude. Treat money as a flowing energy: accept it calmly, let go of it easily and manage it wisely. Do what you love, keep life simple and notice the signs life gives you.

✷ ARCANA 11 ✷

You are here to master your inner power and use it to create, protect and uplift, rather than dominate or destroy. Your task is to believe in yourself, lead with courage and take full responsibility for your life while staying calm, patient and aware. You are meant to turn raw strength and intense emotions into constructive action. Build discipline, care for your body and spirit, replace harmful habits with healthy ones and meet challenges directly. Lead by example, help others without pressure and balance effort with rest.

✷ ARCANA 12 ✷

You are here to practise deep self-love, acceptance and conscious change. Your task is to move out of stagnation without self-sacrifice: rest when needed, trust your ideas and bring your creative talents to life. Your insights matter, and they are meant to be used. You are meant to help others without losing yourself. Set clear boundaries, learn to say 'no', respect your energy and value your work fairly. Release resentment, especially towards yourself, and choose joy over suffering.

✷ ARCANA 13 ✷

You are here to embrace life fully, in all its stages and changes. Your task is to stay curious, learn, explore and constantly renew yourself. Let go of the old clutter, fears and past patterns and make space for freedom, growth and joy. You are meant to adapt gracefully to change, take charge of your own transformation and move forwards without getting stuck. Face challenges with positivity, trust in life and gratitude for what you have.

✷ ARCANA 14 ✷

You are here to connect with your soul, cultivate inner harmony and bring your mind, body and spirit into balance. Your task is to discover and develop your creative gifts and use them to express yourself, help others and even build your livelihood. You are meant to live with moderation, care for your family and find joy in the small, everyday things. Strengthen your body and spirit, practise self-awareness and let go of resentment.

✷ ARCANA 15 ✷

You are here to follow your intuition and grow spiritually while staying on a positive, honest path. Your task is to resist temptations, overcome pride and vices, and avoid harming yourself or others through deceit, conflict or abuse. You are meant to develop awareness, generosity and psychic or intuitive abilities. Pursue your ambitions with integrity, give as much as you receive and cultivate optimism and love.

✷ ARCANA 16 ✷

You are here to awaken spiritually and build a conscious, meaningful life. Your task is to let go of the past, release outdated patterns and create new opportunities for growth in every area: your relationships, work and personal life. You are meant to live with higher goals in mind, transform challenges into progress and maintain clarity of mind and spirit. Through meditation, reflection and conscious action, you can build your life with purpose and integrity.

✷ ARCANA 17 ✷

You are here to develop your talents, shine in your field and follow your unique calling. Your task is to cultivate creativity, self-expression and artistry while turning your passion into success. You are meant to overcome fears and self-doubt, embrace joy and beauty, and maintain a positive, progressive mindset. Build skills, nurture relationships and allow yourself to be seen and celebrated.

✷ ARCANA 18 ✷

You are here to create your reality through your thoughts, imagination and intuition. Your task is to focus on positivity, overcome fears and doubts, and live fully in the present while working towards your future goals. You are meant to develop your creative and intuitive abilities, nurture your home and family and pursue your dreams with clarity and intention.

✷ ARCANA 19 ✷

You are here to be a shining leader, a source of joy, positivity and inspiration. Your task is to cultivate light within yourself, letting go of resentment, ego and rigidity while spreading generosity, prosperity and goodness to those around you. You are meant to direct your energy towards creation, growth and helping others, while maintaining your own flow and self-care. Lead by example, trust life and stay in your personal sunlight.

✷ ARCANA 20 ✷

You are here to strengthen and heal your family, creating harmony, forgiveness and connection across the generations. Your task is to forgive yourself and your parents, resolve family patterns and guide your loved ones with wisdom and love. You are meant to honour your lineage, preserve traditions and build a strong, supportive family of your own. Develop your intuition and ability to sense ancestral and family energy.

✷ ARCANA 21 ✷

You are here to expand your horizons, embrace freedom and connect with the world. Your task is to move beyond limitations, open your mind and approach life with curiosity, tolerance and gratitude. You are meant to dream big, take steady steps towards your goals and enjoy the journey without obsessing over results. Cultivate gentleness, openness and respect for different people, cultures and beliefs.

✷ ARCANA 22 ✷

You are here to live with true freedom, spiritually, creatively and in every area of your life. Your task is to let go of limitations, embrace change and follow your own path with ease, curiosity and joy. You are meant to nurture spontaneity, maintain childlike openness and support your loved ones while fully expressing your creativity. Live freely, travel, explore and approach life with balance, responsibility and playfulness.

YOUR SOCIAL PURPOSE (AGE 40–60)

Tasks for genus, results and recognition in society.

Code:

M: f+y= m
F: g+k= n
m+n= l

Example:

M: 3+15= 18
F: 14+4= 18
18+18= 9*

** Sum totals cannot exceed 22; 36 reduced is 3+6=9*

Your Social Purpose

Here, you calculate the 'M' number from the numbers located at the top and bottom of your father's lineage line, while the 'F' number comes from the numbers at the top and bottom of your mother's lineage line. By adding the sums together, you obtain your social purpose, reflecting how your lineage shapes your interactions and role in the world.

✷ ARCANA 3 ✷

Your social purpose is to create material stability, provide opportunities and share your knowledge, skills and experience with children, employees and your community. You are called to support and guide others, helping them reconnect with any estranged caregivers, and to create stability, prosperity, and well-being in your family and community

✷ ARCANA 4 ✷

Your social purpose is to treat everyone equally, give warmth and respect, and build strong, harmonious relationships. You are meant to develop your professional skills, take responsibility for your actions and use your leadership and influence to create systems, guide others and help people succeed in life and work. You are called to act with fairness, decisiveness and generosity, contribute to the common good and inspire others by example.

✷ ARCANA 5 ✷

Your social purpose is to discover new knowledge and share it with others. You are meant to teach, mentor and guide people through your experience, whether in schools and seminars or as personal guidance. You are called to respect different perspectives, pass on family traditions, heal relationships and create order and freedom in the home. You help others learn, grow and apply knowledge practically, inspiring change by example and keeping your work lawful, fair and constructive.

⁕ ARCANA 6 ⁕

Your social purpose is to learn true love and acceptance of yourself and others, and to help others do the same. You are meant to build harmonious relationships, forgive and embrace people as they are, while creating beauty and joy in their lives. You are called to develop your talents, organize celebrations, foster connections and guide others in understanding themselves and their relationships. You are here to create beauty and bring people together through meaningful connections.

⁕ ARCANA 7 ⁕

Your social purpose is to inspire people to take action, achieve their goals and advance in life. You are meant to teach how to set plans, stay motivated and pursue growth with energy and optimism. You are called to lead teams, organize projects and guide others fairly, recognizing their talents and helping them succeed. Your role is to create meaningful results, spark new ideas and have a lasting positive impact on society.

⁕ ARCANA 8 ⁕

Your social purpose is to understand the deeper patterns of life and share this insight with others. You are meant to act with fairness, wisdom and responsibility, guiding people through complex situations while upholding justice, honour and integrity. You are called to lead by example, showing how to balance laws, morality and compassion, and helping others see the consequences of their actions without judgement.

⁕ ARCANA 9 ⁕

Your social purpose is to use your gift of words and insight to guide and heal. You are meant to listen deeply, offer practical advice and bring clarity and hope to those around you. You are called to develop your foresight and understanding, then step into the world to teach, mentor and lead by example. Your role is to balance knowledge and action, using your influence wisely and responsibly, without pride or control, to make a real difference in people's lives.

✷ ARCANA 10 ✷

Your social purpose is to use your blessings to help others grow and succeed. You are meant to teach people how to live joyfully, work in teams, develop their talents and become independent in life and decisions. You are called to inspire, motivate and guide others by example, showing them how to trust themselves, follow their path and lead a harmonious, fulfilling life. You are here to share your prosperity, wisdom and skills, helping others find happiness, purpose and balance.

✷ ARCANA 11 ✷

Your social purpose is to use your physical and spiritual strength to build, inspire and support others. You are meant to lead by example, manage your power wisely and create projects or communities that benefit many. You are called to mentor, guide and energize people, helping them recognize their talents, achieve their potential and gain confidence, while using your energy and influence wisely.

✷ ARCANA 12 ✷

Your social purpose is to bring kindness, compassion and understanding to others. You are meant to help people see their problems, support them in resolving them and inspire growth. You are called to develop your creativity, serve others without losing yourself and find a balance between your own needs and helping the world. Your role is to share knowledge, offer guidance and create with compassion, bringing new and unconventional ideas and solutions to the world.

✷ ARCANA 13 ✷

Your social purpose is to help yourself and others let go of the old and embrace change. You are meant to transform what is outdated, show people new possibilities and guide them to renewal. You are called to inspire progress, bring joy from chaos and create opportunities for growth and rebirth. You are here to lead change, initiate new projects and help others adapt, keeping life and the world in constant evolution.

✷ ARCANA 14 ✷

Your social purpose is to share your healing experience and help others purify their souls, release their attachments and find fulfilment. You are meant to recognize the good in people, bring harmony to relationships and foster heartfelt connections. You are called to unleash your creativity, show others the beauty of life through art and use your gifts to awaken, heal and inspire.

✷ ARCANA 15 ✷

Your social purpose is to use your gift of clairvoyance to help others heal and grow. You are meant to see the positive in life, guide people to overcome their weaknesses and lead by example with joy, light and compassion. You are called to overcome pride, resist the temptations of money and power, and use your talents to support others with vices or challenges. You are here to lead by example, bringing light, joy and balance to those around you.

✷ ARCANA 16 ✷

Your social purpose is to help people awaken spiritually and see the best in themselves. You are meant to guide others to overcome their fears, weaknesses and destructive patterns, showing them how to build a new life by your example. You help people adapt to change, overcome crises and grow stronger in spirit. Your role is to lead spiritually, helping people grow while finding harmony between material well-being and higher values.

✷ ARCANA 17 ✷

Your social purpose is to help people discover their talents and guide them with your knowledge, intuition and creativity. You are meant to inspire others, lift them from sadness or doubt and show them their path and purpose. You are called to embrace your own creativity, develop your talents and share them with the world so many can benefit. Be a role model and mentor, displaying an open heart and inner harmony.

✷ ARCANA 18 ✷

Your social purpose is to create a positive reality and shape your life with ease. You are meant to think positively, live in the present and overcome fears, doubts and insecurities. You are here to trust your intuition, develop your creativity and use your imagination, style and subtle senses wisely. You are called to focus on opportunities, nurture your home and family, and work towards your goals with clarity and intention.

✷ ARCANA 19 ✷

Your social purpose is to lead, inspire and bring growth and abundance to many people. You are meant to fully express your power, warmth and joy, using your influence wisely to support others and create prosperity. You are here to become a fair and reliable leader who motivates, educates and helps people realize their potential. You are called to bring joy, teach generosity and foster development through large-scale projects, community work and service for the common good.

✷ ARCANA 20 ✷

Your social purpose is to heal and strengthen family bonds by bringing love, forgiveness and understanding into family relationships. You are meant to accept and heal your family lineage, break negative patterns and create a strong, harmonious family as an example for others. You are here to hone your clairvoyant and intuitive abilities to help people understand their family karma, resolve conflicts and find their place and purpose.

✷ ARCANA 21 ✷

Your social purpose is to foster peace, unite people and contribute to global projects that benefit humanity and the planet. You are meant to think globally, learn from other cultures, travel widely and develop skills that allow you to connect people across borders. Through spiritual practice, compassion and service, you can help others expand, heal and grow. You are called to be a citizen of the world – a peacemaker, diplomat and bridge between cultures.

✷ ARCANA 22 ✷

Your social purpose is to live freely and help others to experience freedom in mind, spirit and life. You are meant to awaken awareness and joy within yourself and inspire others through your example. By travelling and staying open, creative and unattached, you can guide people to release limitations, grow spiritually and enjoy life fully. You are called to be a spiritual mentor and pioneer, bringing in healing, optimism, humour and new perspectives.

YOUR SPIRITUAL PURPOSE (AGE 60–80)

Those who have completed their earthly and social duties by around the age of 60 are well placed to move on to fulfil their spiritual purpose and enjoy peace and joy. If the earlier duties have been neglected, shortcomings in worldly and social responsibilities will need to be addressed first.

Spiritual path, global task, where is the divine in me?

Code:

k+l= (o)

Example:

9+9= (18)

Your Spiritual Purpose

Your spiritual purpose is the sum of your personal purpose (see page 157) and social purpose (see page 164). It shows how your inner calling connects with your role in the world, combining your personal growth with your relationships and family influences.

✷ ARCANA 3 ✷

From around the age of 60 onwards, your spiritual purpose centres on creation in the physical world. You are meant to bring ideas, care and fertile energy into visible form, uniting people and resources around something that can grow. When you stay engaged with life, your presence multiplies stability and prosperity for yourself and others. When you withdraw, hide your work or disconnect from the material world, things can unravel and you may be left feeling lost or unsupported. Your path asks you to remain creative and embodied, allowing nurturing energy to take form rather than fade into potential.

✷ ARCANA 6 ✷

From around the age of 60 onwards, your spiritual purpose unfolds through relationships, love and choice. You may be tested by apathy, emotional withdrawal and the urge to close yourself off from the world, but when you resist connection or avoid action, life can feel empty or stagnant. When you choose to stay open, you become someone who transforms relationships through acceptance rather than control. Your path is to move from isolation to unconditional love, allowing your heart to remain open even when the world is imperfect.

✷ ARCANA 9 ✷

From around the age of 60 onwards, your spiritual purpose is to gather your life into wisdom and take it outwards. You are called to share what you have lived, learned and healed, becoming an example rather than a preacher. When you open emotionally and connect spirit with everyday life, your insight helps others find meaning and wholeness. When you withdraw, cling to isolation or avoid responsibility for the past, your wisdom turns inwards and grows heavy. Your path is to heal division within yourself, speak from experience that can help others, and let your lived truth reconnect you with the world.

✷ ARCANA 12 ✷

From around the age of 60 onwards, your spiritual purpose is to become a channel of kindness, insight and connection. You are called to help others through understanding, compassion and the wisdom you've gathered, while also valuing your own energy and boundaries. When you embrace this path, your presence spreads warmth, unity and higher understanding to those around you. When you withdraw, harden your heart or cling to old resentments, your gifts remain dormant. Your path calls for cultivating high-frequency love, sharing your unique talents and guiding others while staying grounded, joyful and fully present in each moment.

✷ ARCANA 15 ✷

From around the age of 60 onwards, your spiritual purpose is to transform life's challenges into clarity, insight and guidance for others. You are called to work through personal blocks, dependencies, addictions and shadows and emerge with understanding and unconditional love. When you face your weaknesses and let go of ego-driven patterns, your presence becomes a source of strength, calm and inspiration. Your path is to rise above inner darkness, cultivate spiritual discipline and share your wisdom with those ready to receive it, becoming a living example of the transformative power of self-mastery.

✷ ARCANA 18 ✷

From around the age of 60 onwards, your spiritual purpose is to bring your unique vision and subtle perception into the everyday world. You are called to embrace your intuitive and magical abilities, seeing connections between the material and spiritual realms that others may overlook. Then your awareness can become a bridge for understanding, healing and guidance. If, on the other hand, you shrink from your gifts or doubt your intuition, opportunities for growth and clarity will slip away. Your path is to use your intuition and understanding of life's rhythms, its timing, cycles and human dynamics, to guide yourself and others, creating real, positive results in everyday life.

✷ ARCANA 21 ✷

From around the age of 60 onwards, your spiritual purpose is to face change head-on and step away from attachments that no longer serve you. You are meant to navigate the tension between old habits, material concerns and the wider world. Your work now is to resolve conflicts, create order where chaos lingers and use your experience to guide others without forcing them. When you resist your calling, you can feel stuck, frustrated or disconnected. Your path is to reflect on your life, spend time in nature and notice patterns in how people and situations unfold so that you can make practical decisions that bring balance to your family, community and surroundings.

CHAPTER 11

YOUR LIFE FORECAST

AGES AND ENERGIES

The numbers below the gold lines circled are your ages, whereas the numbers above are the energies that are in play in those years. To make the most of these influences, aim to stay positive, though this may not be easy, especially when challenges arise despite your best efforts. A more practical approach is to look at the potential negative patterns in your forecast. By noticing where difficulties might appear, you can take conscious steps to avoid, reduce or redirect them, making it more likely that the positive side of the Arcana will show up in your life.

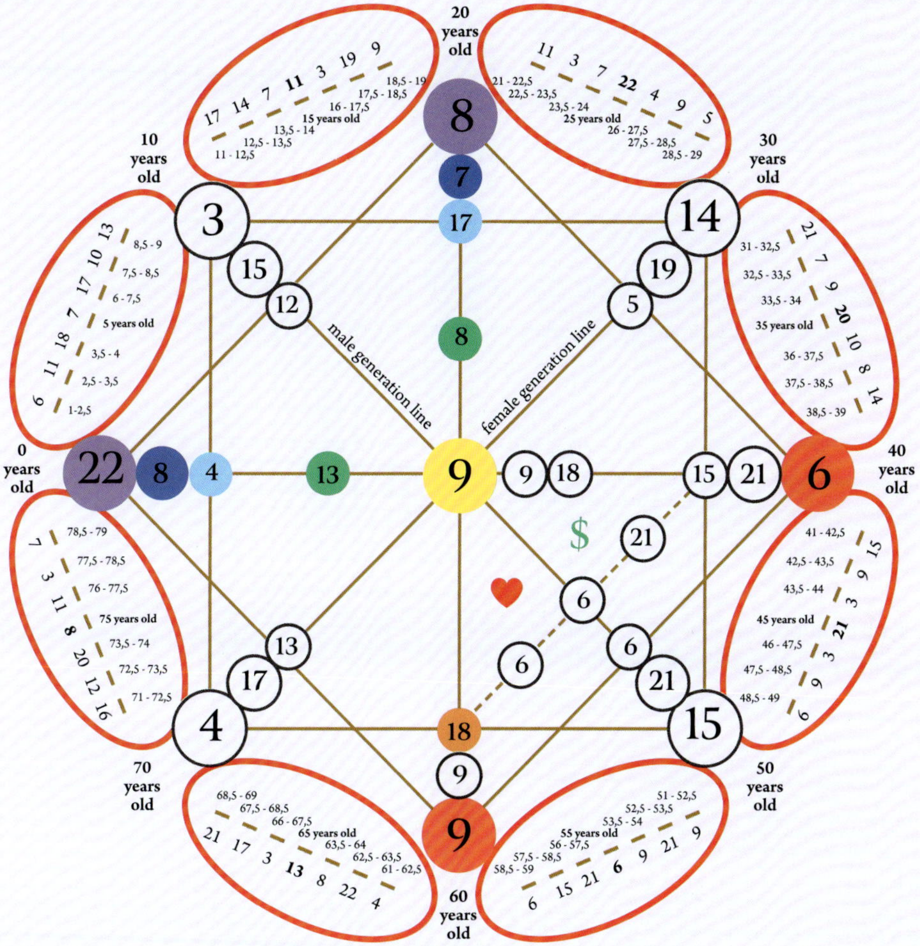

Your Life Forecast

✷ ARCANA 1 ✷

Positive: You may take a short trip, successfully resolve legal matters or paperwork, communicate easily with others and see plans and desires fulfilled. Academic success, new information, spiritual training, learning languages, scientific pursuits, positive events with siblings and the materialization of goals are also possible.

Negative: There may be travel disruptions, document issues or court cases, conflicts, gossip, deception or fraud, problems with studies or false information, inconsistency, negative situations involving siblings, unrealized plans or negative thoughts turning into reality.

✷ ARCANA 2 ✷

Positive: You may experience a good relationship with a maternal figure, pleasant events connected to her, pregnancy or the birth of a child, active spiritual growth, romance, emotional harmony, peace and a generally calm and favourable atmosphere in your personal life.

Negative: There may be conflicts or difficulties related to a maternal figure, problems with children or childbirth, passivity, low energy, irritability, doubts, fears, psychological strain, withdrawal, deception, muted intuition, hidden obstacles, exposure of secrets or risks connected to alcohol, drugs or unhealthy spiritual influences.

✷ ARCANA 3 ✷

Positive: You may experience success in your personal life, love or marriage, the birth of a child, financial profit or achievements related to property, like buying a home. Creative pursuits can flourish, fertility and productivity increase in all areas of life, intimacy brings pleasure and you may feel loved and appreciated by others.

Negative: You may face difficulties in relationships, infidelity or jealousy, problems with pregnancy or children, financial losses, property issues, sexual dissatisfaction or a lack of love and understanding in communication.

✷ ARCANA 4 ✷

Positive: You may experience social and career success, gain a prestigious job or leadership position, advance professionally, increase your income, start or grow a business, achieve ambitious goals and receive rewards for hard work and responsibility. Positive interactions with management, recognition of authority and victory through persistence are also possible.

Negative: You may face work-related problems, conflicts, aggression, the loss of position or power, job loss, business failure, blocked ambitions, demotion, financial losses, difficulties with management, or relationship issues like infidelity or conflict with a partner.

✷ ARCANA 5 ✷

Positive: You may find a mentor or teacher, experience spiritual growth, strengthen your faith, receive help and protection, and feel a sense of peace and support. Marriage or officializing a relationship is possible, as well as positive events involving your family, especially an improved relationship with a father figure and success in studies or teaching.

Negative: You may encounter poor judgement, moral conflicts, the loss of faith or guidance, problems in a marriage, misleading teachers or beliefs, difficulties in higher education, a lack of protection or support, strained relations with a father figure or negative energetic influences.

✷ ARCANA 6 ✷

Positive: You may experience love, new relationships or marriage, make important life decisions, take decisive action and benefit from partnerships. You may enjoy cultural outings, receive gifts, update your style, make new friends, find peace and tranquility, receive help or protection from above, reconcile with others and conclude profitable deals.

Negative: You may face problems in love, infidelity, betrayal, divorce, wrong choices, indecision, broken partnerships, failed deals or contracts, conflicts, loss of friendships, unrest at home, lack of protection, love triangles or interference from third parties.

✷ ARCANA 7 ✷

Positive: You may take a trip or travel, achieve victories and successfully resolve problems, engage in negotiations, experience rapid progress, participate in sports, change jobs, relocate, start a successful business, purchase a car, enjoy overall good luck and possibly get married.

Negative: You may face travel disruptions, conflicts, separation or divorce, failed negotiations, job loss or forced changes, stagnation, business collapse, car accidents or breakdowns, loss, forced relocation, a lack of motivation, the loss of control, addictions, the unexpected disruption or failure of plans or delays in important matters.

✷ ARCANA 8 ✷

Positive: You may see positive outcomes in paperwork, court cases, contracts and transactions. Life can feel stable and balanced, with gradual growth, karmic rewards, fidelity in love, help from officials and inheritance. Honesty, fairness, logic and rationality guide your actions.

Negative: You may face problems with paperwork, court cases, contracts or work, experience stress, deception, revenge from adversaries, karmic punishment, issues with officials or inheritance, internal imbalance, burnout, infidelity, divorce or even imprisonment.

✷ ARCANA 9 ✷

Positive: You may experience slow but steady personal development, study or learning, good relationships with grandparents, retirement, rest and solitude, spiritual growth, finding a teacher, a calm and stable life, wise advice and time for reflection.

Negative: You may face loneliness, divorce, injury, job loss, forced isolation (prison, hospital), poor relationships with grandparents, depression, mental strain, resentment, misunderstanding your desires, pride and an unwillingness to learn or share knowledge.

✷ ARCANA 10 ✷

Positive: You may experience financial success, easy money or winnings, favourable life changes, happy turns of events, a successful trip, job change or promotion, good luck, moving abroad, the end of one cycle and the beginning of another, and karmic rewards.

Negative: You may face money problems, losses or theft, unfavourable life changes, an unlucky turn of events, unsuccessful trips, job loss, forced relocation abroad, stagnation or delays, karmic punishment and the inability to change your circumstances.

✷ ARCANA 11 ✷

Positive: You may experience success and victory, an active and dynamic life, career advancement, recognition and fame, the achievement of goals, business success, creative recognition, excellent health, high energy, passion and a vibrant sex life.

Negative: You may face violence, conflicts, problems in your sex life, attacks by enemies, loss, setbacks, lack of recognition, failed plans, injuries or revenge.

✷ ARCANA 12 ✷

Positive: You may experience spiritual development, necessary sacrifices that lead to a better life, letting go of the past, peace and rest, the calm acceptance of fate, healing, finding faith, helping others, gaining a new perspective on your problems and receiving help from higher powers.

Negative: You may face stagnation, fear of change and obstacles from resisting change, indecision, addiction, false sacrifices, the loss of inner peace or faith, difficult living conditions, self-deception, external deception or involvement with cults.

✸ ARCANA 13 ✸

Positive: You may experience radical changes, transformation, rebirth, major positive personality shifts, healing, liberation from debts or limiting situations, the ending of hopeless relationships, assuming leadership, gaining power, successful surgery and the passing of danger or difficult times.

Negative: You may face a stormy period with injuries, accidents, serious illness or surgery, break-up or divorce, the loss of a loved one, crises, job or financial loss and business collapse.

✸ ARCANA 14 ✸

Positive: You may experience calmness, the timely resolution of matters, faithful and successful relationships, slow but steady personal and career development, stable work, peace at home, inner balance and improvements in health or diet.

Negative: You may face a turbulent period with stress, delays, instability, wasted energy, relationship conflicts, unsuccessful partnerships, constant overwhelm or problems with alcohol, nutrition, or other addictions.

✸ ARCANA 15 ✸

Positive: You may experience success in material matters, financial gain, increased power, career or political achievements, vibrant and passionate relationships and business success.

Negative: You may face danger, violence or crime, addictions, encounters with enemies, magical or energetic attacks, the abuse of power, destructive or sexual addiction-driven relationships, the loss of money or business collapse, self-destructive behaviour and intrigue.

✸ ARCANA 16 ✸

Positive: You may experience a turning-point, begin building something new (literally or figuratively), enjoy stability and protection, advance in your career, be appointed to a leadership position, grow personally, receive unexpected help, successfully resolve bureaucratic matters, purchase land, win a victory or start a life together with a loved one.

Negative: You may face collapse, crises, property problems, drastic changes, blows or injuries, accidents, magical attacks, job loss or divorce.

✷ ARCANA 17 ✷

Positive: You may form new friendships, experience joy, receive powerful support from above, develop spiritually, have strong intuition, enjoy romantic relationships and travel, present your talents publicly, experience life-changing epiphanies, find faith, achieve success, get married and see your hopes fulfilled.

Negative: You may face problems with friends, betrayal, envy, melancholy, the loss of faith or hope, unrequited love, unfulfilled expectations, loneliness, laziness, passivity and sadness.

✷ ARCANA 18 ✷

Positive: You may experience happiness from connections with women, good relations with a maternal figure, creative success, new romantic encounters, peace at home, a focus on your family and children, spiritual growth, pleasant trips and recovery.

Negative: You may face deception, illusions, complicated relationships with women, problems with a maternal figure or children, dangers during travel, stagnation, gossip and envy.

✷ ARCANA 19 ✷

Positive: You may experience joy, success, good health and energy, the birth of a child, a strong relationship with your father, money and power, social recognition, creative achievements and a new exciting romance.

Negative: You may face losses, conflicts, problems with your a paternal figure or other male energies in your life, health or energy issues, financial or creative setbacks, the loss of status and difficulties with children.

✷ ARCANA 20 ✷

Positive: You may experience positive family changes, marriage, the birth of a child, relocation, personal transformation, the realization of abilities, renewal, reaching a new level, the fulfilment of long-standing plans, inheritance, gaining power, the arrival of relatives and karmic rewards.

Negative: You may face family problems, stagnation, resistance to change, unfulfilled development, karmic punishment, prison, serious health issues or mental problems.

✷ ARCANA 21 ✷

Positive: You may experience travel or emigration, the completion of projects, self-realization, peace and harmony, protection from above, the achievement of goals, expanding horizons, success, recognition and popularity.

Negative: You may face travel problems, stagnation, stress, unfinished tasks, a lack of recognition, danger in crowds, falls, imprisonment, the loss of position, negative thinking and helplessness.

✷ ARCANA 22 ✷

Positive: This period may bring a new life stage, opportunities, the birth of a child, new experiences, insights, joy, ease in achieving goals, new friends, spiritual growth, intuition, liberation and successful travel.

Negative: You may face rash decisions, wrong choices, escapism, stress, surprises, accidents, dangerous travel, child-related issues, divorce or the loss of friends.

CONCLUSION

LIVING YOUR DESTINY

When you begin to understand yourself more deeply, life becomes lighter. You stop living on autopilot and start living with awareness – living your destiny.

Spirituality isn't an escape from life; it's a way of living it more fully. It is found in daily choices, in kindness, creativity, gratitude and responsibility.

By understanding your personal Matrix, you gain practical tools to transform challenges, release old beliefs and move into a higher state of alignment with your destiny. Decisions become clearer. Daily challenges feel more meaningful.

Much of your life experience is shaped by what you believe. Your thoughts, emotions and reactions form your faith, and faith shapes reality. When you remain attached to the past, to old wounds, fears or limiting beliefs, you unknowingly recreate the same experiences. But as you shift your beliefs, your reality shifts with you. So, true spiritual work begins with letting go. Forgiveness, self-awareness and conscious inner cleansing make space for new energy, growth and joy.

Change doesn't happen overnight, but every step matters. The journey itself is the reward.

Begin simply. Reduce negativity. Feed your mind with meaningful knowledge. Care for your body. Spend time in nature. Create, move, laugh and rest. Clear your physical and inner space. Practise gratitude. Listen to your intuition. Be patient and gentle with yourself. Remember, even small steps move you forwards. Living your destiny isn't about perfection, it's about awareness, growth and presence. Trust the process. Trust yourself.

And above all, enjoy every moment of your spiritual journey.

BIBLIOGRAPHY

Ashby, M. (2007), *The Kemetic Tree of Life: Ancient Egyptian Metaphysics and Cosmology for Higher Consciousness.* Miami: Sema Institute/Cruzian Mystic Books.

Dale, C. (2015), *Llewellyn's Complete Book of Chakras.* Woodbury, MN: Llewellyn Worldwide.

DuQuette, L.M. (2017), *Understanding Aleister Crowley's Thoth Tarot.* Newburyport, MA: Weiser Books.

Fiebig, J., and Burger, E. (2015), *The Ultimate Guide to the Thoth Tarot.* Woodbury, MN: Llewellyn Worldwide.

Gollov, A.J. (2022), *The Destiny Code Matrix: The Way to the True Self.* Self-published.

Greer, M.K., and Reed, T. (2021), *Archetypal Tarot: What Your Birth Card Reveals about Your Personality, Path, and Potential.* San Francisco, CA: Weiser.

Judith, A. (2015), *Eastern Body, Western Mind: Psychology and the Chakra System as a Path to the Self.* Revised edition. Berkeley, CA: North Atlantic Books.

Jung, C.G. (2013), *Man and His Symbols.* Bowdon, Cheshire: Stellar Classics. (Originally published 1964)

Ladini, N. (2025), *Destiny Matrix* [PDF e-book]. Available at: https://matricaladini.site/pdf_books/tproduct/497941649972-book-destiny-matrix-pdf

— (2025), *Interpretation of Energies According to the Positions in the Matrix of Destiny* [PDF handout]. Handout materials for the First Basic Course. Available at: https://matricaladini.site/matrica_dlya_sebya

— (2025), *Parents and Children* [PDF e-book]. Available at: https://matricaladini.site/pdf_books/tproduct/764178120942-book-parents-and-children-pdf

— (2025), *The Ultimate Guide to 22 Energies* [PDF e-book]. Available at: https://matricaladini.site/pdf_books/tproduct/994566643642-the-ultimate-guide-to-22-energies-pdf

— (2025), *Who You Were in Your Past Life* [PDF e-book]. Available at: https://matricaladini.site/pdf_books/tproduct/503259056442-book-who-you-were-in-your-past-life-pdf

— (2024), *Description of Karmic Tails. Matrix of Destiny Course.* Available at: https://t.me/numerologi_soul/ (accessed: 7 October 2024).

— (2024), *Energies in the Health Map. Matrix of Destiny Course.* Available at: https://t.me/numerologi_soul/ (accessed: 1 October 2024).

— (2024), *Energies of Prognostication. Matrix of Destiny Course.* Available at: https://t.me/numerologi_soul/ (accessed: 1 October 2024).

— (2024), *Finance Channel. Matrix of Destiny Course.* Available at: https://t.me/numerologi_soul/ (accessed: 31 August 2024).

— (2024), *Material Karma. Matrix of Destiny Course.* Available at: https://t.me/numerologi_soul/ (accessed: 4 September 2024).

— (2024), *Professions by Arcana. Matrix of Destiny Course.* Available at: https://t.me/numerologi_soul/ (accessed: 7 October 2024).

— (2024), *Relationship Channel. Matrix of Destiny Course.* Available at: https://t.me/numerologi_soul/ (accessed: 31 August 2024).

PICTURE CREDITS

— (2025), *Sexuality Codes in the Matrix of Destiny. Matrix of Destiny Course*. Available at: https://t.me/numerologi_soul/ (accessed: 14 April 2025).

— (2024), *The Structure of the Matrix of Destiny*. Available at: https://t.me/numerologi_soul/ (accessed: 13 August 2024).

Miller, S. (2017), *The Thoth Tarot: Descriptions, Correspondences, Symbols, and Interpretations*. Self-published.

Nichols, S., and Greer, M.K. (2019), *Tarot and the Archetypal Journey: The Jungian Path from Darkness to Light*. Newburyport, MA: Weiser Books.

Pollack, R. (2019), *Seventy-Eight Degrees of Wisdom: A Tarot Journey to Self-Awareness*. Newburyport, MA: Weiser Books. (Second revised edition originally published Thorsons, London, 1997)

Rod, A. (2024), *The Destiny Matrix*. Columbia, SC: Self-published.

Waite, A.E. (2021), *The Pictorial Key to the Tarot*. New York: Random House. (Originally published William Rider & Son, London, 1910.)

Wang, R. (2001), *The Jungian Tarot and Its Archetypal Imagery*. Stamford, CT: U.S. Games Systems.

— (2004), *The Qabalistic Tarot*. Los Angeles, CA: Marcus Aurelius Press.

Wolf, L. (2010), *Practical Kabbalah*. New York: Harmony Books.

iStock: agsandrew 41, Andrew_Deer 147, AP Chanel 155, AscentXmedia 57, 181, bauhaus1000 175, bingdian 81, ersler 161, Fotolives 185, kyoshino 127, Lara_Uhryn 49, Nick_Pandevonium 7, nikpal 192, Ramziya Abdrakhmanova 15, 112, Samuele Bertoli 187, Shintartanya 23, Sjo 173, Thanunchakorn Rattanakai 99, vovan13 167, Wirestock 111, yupiyan 169; Noun Project: 1art 58, Camilo Farkas 36, Creative Design 104, Eagle Eye 176, Kalaakarini 70, Kalinin Ilya 156, Maria Zamchy 20, ProSymbols 76, Vector Place 136, Veronika Krpciarova 122, Vital Intent 12

Illustrations and Visuals

Illustrations on pages 16, 17, 18 and 19: Canva (Mari) (2024), *Numerologi_soul: Get to Know the Matrix of Destiny*. Available at: https://t.me/numerologi_soul/ (accessed: 13 August 2024); https://www.canva.com/

Illustrations on pages 15, 37, 45, 52, 59, 64, 71, 72, 77, 86, 91, 97, 105, 123, 124, 130, 137, 138, 144, 150, 157, 164, 171 and 177: Canva, Coding Numerology (2024), *Chart Calculator*. Available at: https://codingnumerology-matrix.netlify.app/; https://www.canva.com/

The Rider-Waite Tarot images that appear on pages 22–33 are from designs by Pamela Colman Smith, reproduced from the unabridged Dover 2005 republication of the edition published by William Rider & Son Limited, London, 1911 under the title *The Pictorial Key to the Tart: Being Fragments of a Secret Tradition under the Veil of Divination.*

ACKNOWLEDGEMENTS

I offer my deepest gratitude to my parents, my mother, Devi Kala (Sushma), and my father, Bala Ram, for bringing me into this world and for introducing me to spirituality and faith from an early age. Their guidance, values and unconditional support laid the foundation for the path I walk today.

I am profoundly thankful to the teachers and mentors who have shaped my understanding and practice, especially Natalia Ladini, Mari and Smirnova for imparting their wisdom and knowledge of the Destiny Matrix. Their teachings have been instrumental in the creation of this book and in my personal and professional growth.

My heartfelt thanks also go to my dear friend and astrologer, Sita Rama, for providing the electional dates that supported the timely submission of this book's draft. Her guidance and precision played an important role in bringing this work to completion.

My sincere thanks to Louisa, Lizzie and the teams at Godsfield, and the Octopus Publishing Group, for believing in this work and for giving me the opportunity to bring *Your Destiny Matrix* into the world. I am grateful for their trust, guidance and support throughout this journey.

Above all, I thank the Divine, the universe, my spiritual guides and my ancestors for their constant guidance, protection and inspiration. This book is a reflection of that connection and of the path that I am meant to share with others.

Finally, I extend my gratitude to every soul who has crossed my path, trusted my work and inspired me to continue. This book exists because of you.

With love and gratitude, Kabita.

ABOUT THE AUTHOR

Kabita Giri is a Destiny Matrix expert, numerologist and spiritual guide based between Finland, Nepal and the United States. She specializes in the Destiny Matrix, numerology, Human Design, Tarot and Vedic astrology, blending ancient wisdom with modern insight to help individuals understand their life purpose, karmic patterns and soul alignment.

Known online as @codingnumerology, Kabita has built a global digital community with over 102K followers on Instagram and 183K on TikTok, where she shares educational and intuitive content on self-discovery, destiny and conscious living. Through her online storefront, she offers transformative readings focused on life direction, karma, crisis navigation, soul connections and personal alignment.

Kabita has completed over 10,000 client readings worldwide and is recognized for her clear, grounded and compassionate approach. Her work bridges spirituality and practicality, empowering individuals to live more authentically and intentionally.

She holds a Bachelor of Business Administration in International Business from Turku University of Applied Sciences, Finland, and has pursued extensive professional training across multiple spiritual disciplines. Kabita is a certified Destiny Matrix reader, certified Human Design reader, and certified astrology reader. Her studies include Destiny Matrix studies with Natalia Ladini and Mari, astrological studies with Demetra George and Chris Brennan, Tarot studies with Ernst Wilhelm and Human Design education through Katie Irvine.

Your Destiny Matrix is her debut book, created to help readers decode their energetic blueprint and align with their true path.

codingnumerology
codingnumerology